"Harry Willson has not lost his faith. He has, however moved from credulity to a profound trust in the universe of which he is a thinking part. In this book he celebrates the liberation one achieves by abandoning theism and invites the reader to experience the joy in this freedom. Willson holds the reader's interest with many personal anecdotes."
— Hershey Julien, Ph.D.
U.S. Representative, Sea of Faith

"For many, many individuals, the struggle between honesty and religious indoctrination is a hard one — especially for those of us who were indoctrinated as children. This book should be a great help to anyone wrestling with such problems." — Chaz Bufe,
author of **Heretic's Handbook of Quotations,**
20 Reasons to Abandon Christianity, *et al.*

"For those whose experience of organized Christianity has turned to ashes, Harry Willson provides a fine framework for picking oneself up and dusting oneself off. More important than disenchantment validated is his marvelous call to wonder. He reminds us that if there is grace it must build on nature. And, if there isn't grace, he bravely points to what it means to be deeply human."
— Michael E. Daly, former RC priest
retired professor of Social Ethics at UNM

"I and everyone who reads it will never be the same. ***Freedom from God*** *is at once mind expanding and spine chilling; that's what wonder does. When we view our being in a cosmic, all-inclusive perspective, we are very apt to lose track of where we are... Then 'The only way out is through' becomes a mantra... Willson would persuade us to give ourselves over to the Whole Thing... 'All the multiplicity we see and feel around us is made up of interacting interlocking parts which make up One.' (page 112) The word 'God' is inappropriate in that context because we cannot strip it of its anthropomorphic connotations."*

— Bruce Ferguson, Presbyterian minister, retired
author of **Every Day is Sunday**

*"****Freedom from God*** *is double edged and double sharp. Double edged, because Willson writes both to strengthen the convictions of those who think that the concept of God is outmoded, and to shake the assumptions of those who may still think that the old time religion possesses integrity. Double sharp, because Willson writes with a sharp, ironic mind, and with a sharply pointed 'pen.'"*

— Joseph S. Willis, author of **Finding Faith in the Face of Doubt: A Guide for Contemporary Seekers**

"Where was Harry Willson when I needed him, exploring the mine fields of systematic theology in seminary? If you, the reader, want answers so you can avoid thinking, especially about god-stuff, don't read ***Freedom from God****. But if you want your mind stimulated, don't delay; read this book!"*

— Lee Huebert,
minister emeritus, El Paso Universalist Ass'n
minister emeritus, Otero UU Fellowship, Alamogordo, NM

"Here is a gripping autobiography which begins with a child's 'Sense of Wonder,' what Rudolph Otto called 'The Idea of the Holy,' 'The Numinous,' 'Mysterium Tremendum,' which led historically to the formulation of a traditional concept of God.

"Harry Willson proceeds to describe vividly a life of spiritual/intellectual pilgrimage which leads through formal theological education, an ordination that was disturbing to him, a pastorate that led to a growing sense of alienation from the institution called 'church,' and a stint as schoolteacher.

"Along the way there is a constant grappling with the changing theological scene which reveals him to be a voracious reader with a sophisticated critical sense, and with the social issues of the world as well as the altered life-situations of the people in that world. At the pilgrimage's end he finds himself in a 'post-Christian' position, with a sense of liberation. Gone is his 'God-obsession' and the traditional institutionalization connected with it.

"However, there remains a deep concern for the values and ideals that continue to motivate him, as well as the acknowledgment of the 'Sense of Wonder' with which it all began.

"This professor judges the book to be **required reading for all clergy** *in churches, mosques, and synagogues, as well as* **highly recommended reading for all thinking lay Christians, Jews, and Muslims.** *"*

— Fred Sturm, Ph.D., Philosophy Department, UNM

Dedicated to the Memory
of the Following:

Arius
Nestorius
Peter Abelard
Peter Waldo
John Wyclif
John Hus
Girolano Savonarola
William Tyndale
Martin Luther
Miguel Servetus
George Fox
Roger Williams
Karl Marx
Friedrich Nietsche
Sigmund Freud
Miguel de Unamuno
Erich Fromm
George Santayana

"My atheism, like that of Spinoza, is true piety toward the universe and denies only gods fashioned by men in their own image, to be servants of their human interests."
-- George Santayana, **Soliloquies in England**

Freedom from God

Restoring the Sense of Wonder

Harry Willson

Printed in the United States of America
    First Printing, 2002
    ISBN: 0-938513-33-8
    Library of Congress Catalog Number: 2001 135172

AMADOR PUBLISHERS
P. O. Box 12335
Albuquerque, NM 87195 USA
www.amadorbooks.com

Freedom from God

Table of Contents

Introduction

A. The Sense of Wonder

In the opening pages of **Civilization and Its Discontents,** Sigmund Freud acknowledged the existence, in some people, of what he called "the oceanic feeling." It includes an awareness of one's smallness in the face of the rest of what is. Words like "awe" and "adoration" come to mind. This feeling isn't simply fear, or need not be. It may include a sense of unspeakable joy, a strong feeling of all-right-ness. Often there is an inclination to acknowledge some sort of obligation to do better, or to be better, as part of the awareness of Something.

Freud admitted to having never experienced this feeling personally, but for some reason he felt he needed to refer to it. No doubt he had read of it, and probably he had heard about it from some of his patients. He was a little puzzled by it, and then dismissed it.

In another book, **The Future of an Illusion,** Freud dismisses the "projected father figure" as an illusion, and says it has no future. This is what most people mean by, "God." Freud states that there is nothing to it — there's nothing there; it is simply an illusion.

But the "oceanic feeling" is still there, for some if not all, and it needs additional consideration. Another name for this human experience is "the sense of wonder."

Unlike Freud, this writer has experienced the oceanic feeling, the sense of wonder. My earliest memory of it was a recurring dream, which was more like an audience than a vision. I was very, very young. I heard a voice, calling my name, deep and resonant, compelling, threatening — "Harry! Harry!" It always called the name twice, in Biblical fashion. "Moses, Moses." "Samuel, Samuel." "Saul, Saul." "Harry! Harry!" I waited, trembling, for more. Just my name, and a compelling feeling that I had to do something, that I was not all right, that I was leaving something undone, or that I had done something wrong.

That Voice poisoned childhood. I have had to go back and recover as an adult the spontaneity and freedom and joy that the story-myths attribute to childhood. I have more "fun" now than I ever had as a child, and far more joy. Being a tormented child meant that life was all work and obedience and disobedience and trouble and weakness and misunderstanding and confusion and ignorance.

Much later I became convinced that that voice was a psychological mechanism, my father's authority internalized very early. Psychoanalysts would have called it The Super Ego. But I, and everybody around me, called it "God," and I had to take it seriously. It cost half a lifetime to break free.

But the oceanic feeling persists, even though the Voice has been unearthed and aired, and understood and removed. I have felt the sense of wonder many times, and now I deliberately seek that special awareness. I have come to believe it is a good thing.

As a child I sought it in the church, since it was assumed by everyone around me that the Source of that sense of wonder was to be found there. I joined in the pretence, willingly and eagerly at first, and then with more and more difficulty. The oceanic feeling did not come the day I was baptized. The water dried during the sermon and I felt no different. It didn't come in the communion services, with the trays of bread and the tiny glasses of grape juice. It did not come the evening I was ordained a "minister," even though I wanted it to very much. I could not force that sense of wonder to operate, by praying or preaching or reading the Bible or listening.

I could not force it, but from time to time it came to me anyway. It was always a surprise. I fully appreciated the title of one of C. S. Lewis' books, **Surprised by Joy**.

On one occasion, I was camping as a boy with a friend, and awakened by a strange light. It was not the moon, which was over there. This was another light over that other way, in the meadow. I sat up and pulled my glasses from my shoe and put them on. Could a car be coming on that steep narrow rut-track, in the dark in the middle of the night? No, it was not that kind of light, and the woods were silent.

We tried to walk quietly among the dried fallen leaves, but could not. We stopped at the edge of the meadow. "God Almighty!" my companion blurted, with a gasp. For an instant, I thought of stories of angels and holy light, but I could tell this was different, and this was not a story.

A cloud of light hovered at the far end of the meadow, moving inside itself, as high as the trees in some places, but mostly not taller than a boy. It grew as we watched it.

The cloud sent out sections of itself along the edge of the meadow, into the trees, then pulled back, then extended further, taking over more and more space.

"It's coming this way!" my friend whispered, sounding scared.

"Yeah. What is it?" I asked.

"I dunno, but I think we should get outa here," he said.

"Not me. I wanta see what it is." We were whispering loudly, and the cloud of light was approaching. I was not exactly afraid. I was excited. I felt something, all right, but not fear. My heart pounded, and I could hear myself panting, as if I had been running. But I couldn't run away, and didn't want to. "Let's see what it is."

I studied the moving, growing, approaching cloud of light. I saw little points of light inside the big glow. Each one blinked on and off, as I watched. The blinking was especially plain out on the growing edges of the cloud.

The expanding arm of the mass of light came nearer to us. "I think I'm gonna go," my companion said, with a tremble in his voice.

"O.K.," I said, meaning, "You go if you want to. I'm staying."

I stood my ground. As the cloud approached close enough for me to reach out and touch it, I saw what it was. I had seen them before, but never by the millions. Fireflies. "Lightning bugs," we kids called them. But millions of them. They landed on my arm, and blinked on and off. They went on past me. They were circling the meadow, and crossing it, and filling it. I stepped out onto the grass, and felt myself surrounded by all those gentle little bits of light. At the same time, the whole cloud felt to me like something very big, very powerful, irresistible.

I didn't know what to make of it. Magic, weird, perfectly natural, very strange, exciting, breath-taking — I sat down in the meadow and let the lightning bugs play on me. I lay down and looked up through the cloud of light. They hid the stars. The light went deep into my eyes and did something to my insides. I stayed lying there for hours. I must have fallen asleep. When dawn changed the color of the sky, the cloud was gone.

The following winter, on a bitter cold night when my folks were worrying about the danger of the water pipes freezing, an uncle came visiting. He came on the coldest night of the year to bring the family a bushel of pecans from Florida. He greeted the grown-ups, delivered the pecans, and then turned to me. "Get a sweater on, and then your coat. Also a hat, and good mittens."

"Where we goin'?" I asked.

"Outside. I want to show you something."

We went out. It was very dark. The shoveled snow was piled up taller than I between the street and the sidewalk. The temperature was below zero.

We stood in the middle of the street on the packed snow and looked up. The sky had changed. Curtains of light hung down, from overhead, all the way to the north end of Arch Street. Moving sheets of color — purple, green, dark red, pink, silver. The lines of color moved like draperies opening and closing, lifting and falling.

I was stunned. My heart pounded. My voice sounded little and far away. "What is it? What's happening?"

"I'll explain later," said my uncle in a hushed voice.

After the first exclamations and questions, we both were silent. It looked like the entrance into Heaven. I stood there with my head craned back for a very long time, soaking it in. I was having a vision, better than Jacob's ladder. The curtains opened, inviting me to come up and in. They closed. They opened again. It was like a call to come up and in.

At last my uncle pulled me back down and away from that mystery, back into the house. While the family worried about the effect of the extreme cold, most of me was somewhere else. In the sky. In "Heaven."

My uncle taught me the words, "Aurora Borealis." He didn't think "Northern Lights" was good enough. And I was glad for the strange words. Really magic words, they were, for something marvelous and precious and totally mysterious.

The Aurora Borealis had no noticeable effect on the rest of the family, that I could notice. But it had done something to me. I could tell. It was like the previous summer's cloud of fireflies. Something. Something. The Whole Thing, maybe. Not our insignificant little sins. Something big and important and alive and powerful and gentle. I knew something I didn't know before, and was glad. I couldn't put it into words, maybe, but I knew. Something.

It was the sense of wonder. I felt it again as a teen-ager on my first airplane ride, looking down on my home town.

I felt it later, looking into a child's face as she died.

I feel it when I am swept away by sexual ecstasy.

I feel it, sometimes, as I kneel alone staring into the

fire in the little fireplace in our living room.

I have felt it reading certain books, discovering new, previously unimagined continents.

And I feel the oceanic feeling every time, when, after an absence of months or years, I first see again the ocean itself. I wallow in that feeling, when I play in the surf.

The oceanic feeling is not always pleasant. Littleness is part of it. Helplessness often is. A sense of loss of control, along with fear and frustration, can be in it. An awareness of my mortality is in it.

I must state again that I have never felt it in church, although I sometimes joined in the pretence that we did.

I have observed that those who use the word "God" most glibly are usually very arrogant and unpleasant persons. TV evangelists, for example, and leaders of extremist political and religious movements. "God" can become an excuse and even a justification for plain old nastiness.

On the contrary, the oceanic feeling, the sense of wonder, can lead people to a humble awareness of Truth, with some sense of the human ego's relative size and importance, in all the Cosmos. More gentle and more loving human beings can be the result. I don't believe we want to get rid of the sense of wonder.

The sense of wonder, felt when looking through telescopes or microscopes, or into the heart of a volcano, or into the eye of a friend, does not require a Transcendent Entity, a projected personification of ego's fear.

The sense of wonder can enhance life greatly, rather than terrify or stifle and regulate, when it is arrived at from looking inward. All that power and order, and the

wonder they inspire, are within. What transcends ego,
which is something ego badly needs, is not Omnipotent,
Omniscient, Wholly Other, but rather the connectedness
of What is Within to the Innerness of all things. What is
in me is in all, in us all, as well as volcanos and galaxies.

A restored sense of wonder can become an invitation
to an inward journey. Let us confront the infantile fear, so
easily projected outward as "the fear of God." Let us find
the strange powerful unknown within each one, and make
peace with that. Then we won't need an Entity "out there"
to explain and justify things, from which we must then
seek forgiveness. Let's go on in and find out how
marvelous each one is, and how connected we are to
everything else. Inner Peace comes, not from tricks of
sacrifice that mollify an angry Entity that we have
offended, but rather from accepting all the parts of
ourselves. We'll find them inside there.

Scholars of the anatomy of the human brain have
begun to identify that portion of the organ which deals
with mysticism, mythology and mystery. There is plenty
of mystery to be dealt with — "Where'd we come from?"
"Where are we going?" "What the Sam Hill is going on
anyway?" Sometimes these are called "philosophical
questions," and there are people who push them away as
soon as they come up. Others go for pre-packaged
answers to such questions without really putting to use this
mystery organ which we all have.

The wonder organ, that section of the brain that senses
wonder, or is in play when wonder is sensed, can be
located in all of us and therefore must have had some kind
of evolutionary advantage in past eons. Just thinking about

that in itself will put your wonder organ into motion. What is it for? What survival function does it serve? Why did it evolve at all?

Which leads to the next question — does the existence of this organ correspond to something "out there?" We have eyes because there is light out there and our eyes use light to perceive what else is out there. We have ears because there is sound, and our ears use sound to help us perceive what else is out there. So — do we have the wonder organ because there is Something out there? Something that would help us perceive Something Else?

Well, there is no question that there is something there all right — all that Mystery, the Unknown, the Incomprehensible, the Indescribable. Some philosophers call it "the numinous." When your wonder organ is working, you're in touch with That. Right away someone is going to want to call it "God," but that will amount to short-circuiting a process that would do more good if allowed to work further without resorting to that word. It would be like taking a shortcut too soon. Jumping to "God" very well may shut down the wonder organ before it has had a chance to do much or learn much or grow much. If you watch carefully, you'll find that religions tend not to be much help in this wonder department, even though that's what they pretend to be all about.

When one looks carefully over the eons, one observes that the function of the religions for the most part, so far, has been to harness, channel, control, not to say stultify, mediocritize and asphyxiate, that sense of wonder or mystery that we are dealing with here. Religions channel ecstasy into pageantry. They trade conviction for tradition.

Religions are designed to make saints out of advanced wonderers, like Francis of Assisi or Teresa de Avila. The effect is to put their example out of reach. We're supposed to admire and even worship them, rather than do what they did or what they taught. Religious organizations prefer to control people, rather than turn them on to wonder, which will turn them loose, or make them free.

But wonder keeps turning up, overthrowing the way the social system wants us to think. The wonder organ can help us know, really know — and then the spin-doctors appear in our eyes as users of falsehood and deception. We'll search for causes rather than cures, for things like cancer, and then it'll be harder for the perpetrators of the causes to keep us in line.

The sense of wonder, turned loose, can make us reach further and change our minds and even change what we've been doing. The sense of wonder, and our wonder organs, could make our lives so exciting, so vibrant, that it would become unthinkable that we would permit the life-hating forces and powers of religion to spoil everything.

So, the wonder organ is an evolutionary advantage. We, all together, need to exercise it well just now, because the species happens to be in considerable danger, and all the easy speeches that comfort cruel men aren't helping. Our wonder organs will make Freethinkers of us, if we let them. We will then be regarded as subversive and dangerous, a threat to the comforts and advantages that those who would destroy the world now obtain from their activities. It'll take courage, but it'll be exciting, and worth doing.

◊   ◊   ◊

B. Another Obsession

Many of the support groups which are so popular these days are designed to help persons become free of some obsession. Alcohol, nicotine, pills, food, sex, work — whatever. The abuse of any of these things constitutes a problem, and the idea is that persons who have identified a common problem can often help each other.

This book is concerned about becoming free of still another obsession. It is more harmful and more painful than others, because it is not generally recognized as an obsession at all. The freedom being sought is generally regarded by others as a loss. "She lost her faith," someone will say. She may feel better, and be obviously better off, but the general attitude toward her, which she must learn to put up with, is that something unfortunate has happened.

The professor was explaining to his students the function of a priest, any priest in any religious system. He named two functions:

[1] to sanction whatever society is doing, in the name of a Higher Power, and

[2] to placate the numinous. He was asked to explain number two without jargon. "Get God off our backs," he said. Sacrifices, offerings, prayers, holy obligations, fasting — whatever it takes to get "God," or whatever gods may be, to leave us in peace. "They'll pay

you, a little," he growled, "and expect you to relieve them of 'God'."

Then he shifted topics and began to explain the function of a prophet. That was the title used in ancient Israel, although other cultures and religions have other names for them. "The gadfly that stings," Socrates called himself. "Agents of cultural change," is a phrase used today, to refer to some artists. The prophet sees what's going on, applies some overarching standard to it, like Justice or Truth, or what he understands to be "the will of God," or "the word of God," and then he sounds off.

But, said the professor, just as the prophet gets going, "here they come with those damned rattles." Here they come, not interested in the prophet's objections to what society is doing. Here they come, demanding that the priest quit referring at all to "social issues" and return to his task, which is to get God off their backs.

I tried to be a sort of prophet, long ago, but didn't handle well at all the role of priest. I never got "God" off other people's backs at all. But now, unconnected to any ecclesiastical organization, I find I have gotten "God" off my own back, and wonder if what I've learned could help someone else figure out how to do it, too. So, I write this.

The dictionary defines an obsession as "a persistent idea, desire, emotion or pattern of behavior, especially one that cannot be got rid of by reasoning." We have a right to be concerned about those obsessions that make a person do things that are harmful to oneself or others.

"You smoke too much" — it'll kill you, and injure those around you.

"You drink too much" — it'll kill you, and interfere

with work and family meanwhile.

"You can't get sex under control" — it's ruining your life, and other people's.

"Your work has become an obsession" — it'll kill you, and meanwhile leaves no time or energy for any of the rest of your life.

"God" in the minds and in the lives of many is a sort of obsession, which leads them to believe things which are foolish and patently not true, and to do things which are unwise and unkind, both to others and to themselves.

A mental or emotional disability is different from a physical one. You adapt to the physical and go on as best you can. Eyeglasses, dentures, wooden legs, wheelchairs, limps — you adapt. An obsession/disability is something to get rid of, if possible, because it makes you do unwise things. For example:

[1] "God" may lead you to thwart your desires.

[2] "God" may lead you to set aside your own best interests.

[3] "God" may lead you to feel guilty for things you didn't do.

[4] "God" may lead you to feel guilty simply for being the way you are.

[5] "God" may lead you to think more highly of yourself than you ought to think.

[6] "God" may lead you to think more lowly of yourself than you ought to think.

[7] "God" may lead you to stay aloof from fine people.

[8] "God" may lead you to meddle where you have no business.

[9] "God" may lead you to approve of nonsense.

[10] "God" may lead you to approve of wickedness.

Very much of that kind of thing can mess up life badly. Individuals can change, however, especially when they want to.

"I can't handle this any more. It's beyond my control. I know it doesn't make sense, but I can't stop myself. I need help." There is already in existence a Fundamentalists Anonymous organization, designed to de-program people from fundamentalist Christian cults. Perhaps there is need of an even wider-reaching movement. God Anonymous, offering help in getting rid of the God-obsession.

If "God" — whatever definition one may be using, whether deliberately or by default — feels like a disability and a hindrance to a full life, then this discussion may be helpful. If there are forbidden topics in one's mind and conversation, unthinkable points of view, unimaginable companions or friends because of what they believe or even what they look like, it may be the "God"-obsession which is hindering the fullest sort of experience.

"God" may be an ogre left-over from childhood training, which still troubles the nightmares of an adult. If that's so, it can be understood and outgrown.

Having noted that, it is necessary to be aware that there is a risk here. After probing into all this, defining "God" more carefully, at last, and noting some of the remarkable history of the idea, there is the danger that the seeker will decide that everything humans have ever meant by the term is nonsense, and everything they have ever done in the name of "God," is worse than nonsense. There is no doubt that a great deal of very bad behavior and very harmful teaching has been justified by appealing to "God." But one can over-react.

The danger is that the inner search, the quest for meaning in life, the sense of wonder, and the seeker's response to the sense of wonder will all be rejected, in the name of one's personal freedom from this far-reaching obsession.

We want freedom, and clarity and truth, but when we find them, we want them to enhance the sense of wonder. There is a great deal to wonder about, with or without "God." The quest, the search for meaning, does not need "God" to justify itself. We are trying to root out an obsession, not our remarkable ability to wonder about life and the world we are a part of.

C. Self-aware

"Is The Cosmos self-aware?" I asked.

"Surely it is," the philosopher replied.

"I suspect it may be," I said, and then added, to myself, some of the following:

By pondering the arrangement of things and the known rules of that arrangement, and imagining the myriad unknown rules of the same arrangement, I find myself supposing that The Cosmos may be self-aware. It does contain some aware entities, you and me, for starters. It contains at least a kind of partial self-awareness.

Even if the Cosmos *is* self-aware, we should not call that self-awareness "God," because that word conjures up too many notions that range from the preposterous to the wicked, and we'll waste much energy having to refute what no longer needs refuting.

Teilhard de Chardin knew all that, and allowed the Pope and the Jesuits to keep the word "God," while he went on, and left them scratching their heads in utter perplexity as to what he meant by his far-stretched notions, like Point Alpha and Point Omega. I'll admit that his ideas are far from crystalline in their clarity, but he was trying. He was hindered by a strange loyalty to the Pope and the Jesuit Order. I am grateful that I am not.

Who else is not hindered by philosophical axioms and

theological presuppositions, but still willing to wonder about The Cosmos? Is The Cosmos just? Does it care about Justice, really, or is that idea nothing more than a deceptive ploy on the part of the powerful to justify their own misdeeds? Is The Cosmos stupid? Is The Cosmos fooled by our rationalizations and explanations and excuses and sacrifices and rituals and atonements of one kind or another?

Could those of us who still want clarity on this matter ever find each other, or must it always be a loner here and a loner there, calling out like crickets in the night, chirping but not finding each other, not hearing each other, longing for someone to share the quest but questing nevertheless, with or without a group? I needed to become free of "God." My own liberation now seems like such a marvelous wonder that it impels me to turn back to those still imprisoned and say, "You, too, can be free! You can repudiate that authority, and remove those fingers at your throat. You can breathe!" To those who have instinctively insisted on breathing rather than choking, I want to say, "You don't need to feel bad about 'betraying' that which held you prisoner. Be glad and proud that you're free."

All of you who are not imprisoned, hindered, hampered, hobbled, hamstrung, or wing-clipped by "God" — ignore me. You're the lucky ones, and you can go your way without hesitation. I'm looking for those who want loose, who want out, who want to fly, to run, to sing, to dance, to say what you're thinking, to say, "No!" because that's the honest thing to say. And I'm looking for the others who have found their way out, one way or another, and may be feeling a little scared and bewildered out here in the fresh air.

I need to warn you, those around you will say you're going crazy. That's what going sane and free looks like from inside the prison. It'll take courage, but it'll be worth it.

Do you feel at home in The Cosmos? Or do you think "God" is after you, watching you, snooping, prying, objecting to your pleasure, binding heavy burdens on you, obligating you? It's a trick that has been played on you, by parents, siblings, neighbors, teachers, peers, authorities — to make you know your place and stay in it. When you're ready, you can wise up, and take charge of your own life.

Now, having gotten that far, can we go back to the original question? Is the Cosmos self-aware? Does our own curiosity about the inner, the mysterious, the connections between aware persons, the way our own consciousness can reach and stretch — does any of that mean anything? I think it might, if we can get past the pat little pre-arranged assumptions and answers.

D. On Getting over the Past

I have felt a great deal of shame and bitterness about the past. No, I'm not an ex-felon. I never robbed or murdered anyone. I am an ex-clergyman and an ex-missionary. I used to pretend that I knew about things which no twenty-five-year-old could possibly know. I used to try to counsel people in trouble — alcoholics, people near death, people in grief, people in collapsing marriages, mentally ill people, heart-broken people, people who were angry or frightened or proud or greedy or nasty or mean-hearted, — as if I wasn't in trouble enough myself, as if I had answers to their questions and solutions to their problems.

My wife told me the other day that the only thing in her full life that she's ashamed of is her former connection to the church, how she used to believe all that and take it seriously and really try to act out the doctrines and the teachings. I feel plenty of that, too. All the arrogance, all the judgmental evaluation of what was really other people's business, all the interference, all the stupid waste of energy and time and concern — I also feel shame just remembering those things.

But now it must be let go. What is done is done. A person has to start from wherever he is. I had to do that then, and I have to do it now, and so does everyone.

What is to be done now is to understand it better, be wiser because of it — and let it go.

I really want to be rid of the arrogance. I'm ready to mind my own business. It's time, and past time, to tend to my own life, which is the only thing I can legitimately change in any way anyway and the only thing for which I am fully responsible.

And I want to give up the regret over wasted energy. Sometimes I feel plain foolish, remembering what I did and tried to do, as a person seriously trying to do what I thought "God" wanted. I suppose everyone my age feels some of that foolish regret, God or no God. We have to let it go.

I watch, with considerable envy, the kids wasting energy, working off energy, seeking ways to exhaust themselves. I find myself wanting to do some energetic thing, but I arrive at exhaustion sooner than I used to. Maybe I'm trying too hard to recover the shattered dreams of childhood that I never really had then. I was a victim of what some of us now call "spiritual abuse."

The First Big Question was disallowed, for instance. "What do you want?" It never came up. The shattering of the dreams of childhood was impossible, because there weren't any. I got over it, at last, in the second half of this strange journey. I began to dream, but not until after I got rid of "God." The great obsession poisoned the first half of life.

An old verse comes back, and means more than ever. "You shall know the truth and the truth shall make you free."

◇   ◇   ◇

I. The Great Obsession

We need to rescue myth from The Great Obsession. We need to get rid of that obsession or it'll be the end of us. But we can't get rid of myth, of mystery, of infinity, of choice, of causation, of responsibility for previous actions, of memory, or the magic of true friends and a shared life.

The Great Obsession is "God" — or rather the human belief that there is a God, an Entity who made the world, who owns it and operates it, who is in charge of what happens in it, who selects certain people to be related to him in a way different from people generally, who makes demands of all people and special demands of the special people, whose demands are impossible to meet, who condemns, who demands sacrifice, who forgives and makes fresh demands on those forgiven.

This great obsession hinders personal development and the growing of an authentic self from the inside. The self will inevitably be inclined to be disobedient and will be accused of selfishness. Any who believe that this disobedience is a bad thing will find their own lives badly hampered and will almost surely participate in the condemnation and disdaining of all the other people nearby, who are busy trying to live their own lives. We need to examine this great obsession in more detail, and let history and reason help put it into perspective.

A. On Approving Wickedness

A remarkable quantity of criminality has been sanctioned and approved and even encouraged over the centuries — in the name of "God."

The ultimate expression of human madness and violence, that is, armed conflict without rules — wars of all kinds, declared and undeclared, covert and overt, with all the unspeakable cruelty and destruction — this has been declared permissible and even "just," for many centuries by both participants and observers, in the name of "God."

According to the story, Joshua invaded Canaan, at YHWH's behest, and conquered, and slaughtered everything in his path in a genocidal clean sweep. When something less than total annihilation of the defeated enemy men, women, children and cattle was allowed in an exceptional case, YHWH violently disapproved and withheld support for the next battle, which resulted in disaster for Israel. "God" was demanding nothing less that total genocide.

A couple of centuries later the scribes assert that YHWH assisted David in the formation of a huge Israeli empire by military conquest, held together by military force and occupation.

Several centuries later several of the prophets declared that "God" had changed sides, and delivered Israel into the hands of the Assyrian conqueror, Sennacherib. The reason given was that Israel had not been faithful in the worship of YHWH. Later, according to the interpretation of events given by the prophet Jeremiah, "God" assisted Nebuchadnezzar of Babylon in the conquest of Jerusalem.

In the early fourth century, A.D., "God" assisted a Roman general, Constantine, enabling him to win, by force of arms, the position of Roman Emperor. "God" used wholesale slaughter to make Christianity the official religion of the Roman Empire.

"God" and Christ enlisted knights and soldiers and even children, to march to the Near East and kill and be killed in an effort to take the so-called Holy Land by force from persons who were not Christian. Much of the maniacal anti-European and anti-American feeling in that same territory today is the pent-up retaliatory response. Nothing begets terrorism better than terror, and if "God" is brought into the picture, first on one side and then the other, reasonableness inevitably has trouble being heard.

"God" recruited priest/soldiers, who robbed, slaughtered and enslaved the peoples of huge empires in Mexico and Peru. The violent destructiveness of the God-obsessed wiped out the art and science and finally even the written languages of the losers. All this destruction of beauty and knowledge, and human life, was done in the name of "God" and Truth and Love. Since those conquests, the theft of wealth, minerals, sugar, coffee, rubber, and soil fertility has continued without ceasing.

Puritan preachers in New England gave special thanks to "God" for plagues of measles and small pox which spread from the whites to the natives and exterminated whole tribes in time to open their land for "settlement."

Slavery and genocide predominated in the establishment of the new experiment in "self-government" in the Western Hemisphere. The inferiority of the victimized colored races was regarded as something "God" had arranged, and was widely preached and believed at the time — and still is.

Because of Manifest Destiny, that is, the gift from "God" of the whole central swath of North America to the white invaders, wars of conquest in the name of "God" took the U.S. Marines all the way to the Halls of Montezuma, in order to secure the theft of more than half the land mass of Mexico.

The British took over one-fourth the land mass of the entire globe, in the name of "God" and the crown, convincing most of the population of the planet that "God" is a special weapon in the hands of white people.

In our century, obliteration bombing of whole cities was justified, in the belief that "God" fights on America's side and approves of whatever horror the Americans can devise for the destruction of their opponents.

The build-up of sufficient nuclear warheads to destroy the very biosphere itself many times over in the name of "liberty," is widely seen as an act of obedience to "God." He requires us to defend ourselves, it is believed, and it would be better to end altogether the experiment of life forms on this planet rather than let atheists who do not believe in "God" have any say in anything. This is not only wickedness, to prepare to destroy the planet itself, it is also madness. Where were the destroyers planning to live after they finished?

This nonsensical wickedness proceeds apace, and many

persons obsessed by "God," some in high places, believe in the myth of Armageddon, the last battle between good and evil. There is one reference to Armageddon in the Bible, in the Book of Revelation. The language is mythical, describing angels, dragons, a beast that is part leopard, part bear and part lion, with ten horns and seven heads. Three foul spirits like frogs issue from the mouths of the dragon, the beast and the false prophet. The frogs go abroad to the kings of the whole earth, to assemble them for battle, and they gather at Armageddon for the last clash. That's all it says.

Armageddon may be a real place — the Plains of Megiddo, in Israel, where King Josiah met his untimely end, killed in battle in the year 608 B.C. by Pharaoh Neco of Egypt. Josiah allowed himself to be called away from serious and encouraging reforms which he had earlier initiated, seduced tragically into geopolitics and war.

That reference to Megiddo is ancient history. The rest of the story in Revelation is myth, and not at all clear. To call those references to dragons and frogs "prophecy" about current events is nonsense. And to take this particular myth of Armageddon literally at all is evil. But persons obsessed by "God" are doing just that. To accept the idea of, to believe in, and then to prepare for, the destruction of the entire world in fiery violence — it is wickedness.

These people believe that the World is evil and that it is full of evil people, who deserve to be destroyed. Most of the inhabitants of the planet are to be sure non-white and anti-American, but that alone doesn't make them evil. It is evil self-hating nonsense to believe that they all

deserve to be incinerated. Maybe the author of the Book
of Revelation believed that. If so, his way of following
and obeying the Prince of Peace was pathetically and
pathologically twisted into a life-hating, world-hating,
orgy of imaginary destruction. It is still evil nonsense, and
far more dangerous now than when he first wrote it,
because now it is possible to bring about what he
envisioned.

The power to bring about all that destruction is in our
time not a myth. It is a literal fact, many times over. It is
madness, also. To destroy a planet is evil madness. To
approve of it, to get ready to do it, to help pay for getting
ready to do it, to "upgrade" and "keep in dependable
readiness" the instruments by which it can be done — all
that is taking part in the same evil madness.

There is no "God" who wants to destroy the world.
Some humans, in their pathological unthinking hateful
cynicism, may want to destroy the world. We ought not
depend on a supernatural "God" to stop them. You and I
must stop them. And, sooner or later, and sooner would
be better than later, we'll have to dismantle all that
weaponry which makes this myth something to take
seriously. We may as well get at it.

Backing away, for another view of all this, we see that
the systematic, piecemeal destruction of the natural world
has characterized from the beginning the expansion of this
culture which we call "western." It is a culture obsessed
with "God." Another myth is at the root of the motivating
attitude. "God" gave the world to man, to subdue, the
story says. "God" gave man superiority over the beasts,
making extinction of species no crime. God gave man the

forests and the sea, the mountains and the prairies, to exploit, buy, sell, divide, fight over and destroy.

The comparatively new ecological awareness — that Life is all one organism, not a plaything of humanity but a destructible, fragile characteristic of this very unusual planet — such ideas have a difficult time burrowing into people's heads and hearts, because the obsession with "God" tends in the opposite direction, feeding man's inclination to be proud and selfish and thoughtless and stupid and mean.

From still another angle, we may say that cruelty to children has been perpetrated in the name of "God." Adults obsessed by "God" want to thwart that spontaneity, control that freedom, harness that innate honesty and truthfulness, hem in that curiosity, "spiritualize" that sensuality, spoil the pleasures, add to the fears, exaggerate the weakness and littleness, teach duty and guilt.

The process creates adults who have fears to get over, unreasonable feelings of obligation to puzzle out, up-tight attitudes toward their own bodies and other people's, difficulty smiling or touching or enjoying, guilt about success or good fortune, expectations of trouble and misery and illness and incompetence.

The ultimate wickedness, in one's own personal life, is cruelty to self. The victim tends to blame himself or herself, thus making whatever else is the matter worse. Or an adult may be nursing belated hostility, which hampers life now. In my case I raged, deep inside, late in life, against my father. Not as a child — that was unimaginable and totally impossible then. But later, when I saw what had been done, and how unfair it was, I was furious —

and still no better off.

In my case I began to feel better when I admitted to myself that I allowed it, and that pleading weakness and littleness did no good. The important new development was that I was no longer weak and little, and did not need to allow cruelty any more. To the extent that I still continued to allow it, it was my own doing, and cruelty to self, which needed to be stopped.

An adult can understand it, and then put a stop to it. If the perpetrators of the cruelty will not stop, one can get away, out of their reach, and then outlive them. One is not required to let them use "God" to persecute adult victims. And one dare hope that those who have figured this out will not be inclined to use "God" as an excuse for cruelty toward anyone else.

B. The Will of God

Children in Sunday Schools, adolescents in youth groups, and adults listening to sermons are often challenged and troubled by the question, "What is God's will for my life?" The chanted statement of purpose of the youth group I was part of long ago was quite ominous, looking back on it. "... to discover God's will for our lives, and do it."

Each one subjected to this teaching is asked to believe that "God" created him or her, and put him or her here for a specific purpose. The task laid on us was to discover what that purpose was. Individuals were often perplexed by the fact that "God" hid his purpose so well, making each one of us unsure, requiring each one to dig and ponder and wonder and squirm and puzzle over it.

The hiddenness of the supposed purpose should have been a clue, but often it wasn't. "If God wants me to do something, why doesn't he say what? Why would he tell Dad, or the minister, instead of me? I'm the one who will have to do it finally." Instead, that uncertainty became part of the problem, making obedience harder. Perhaps I suffered on account of this uncertainty more than some others subjected to the same teaching.

I felt called to obey, but didn't know what God's will for my life was. Finally I made up answers to that question, and then persuaded myself that they came from "God." I then proceeded pell-mell with admirable single-mindedness and remarkable stupidity to execute the imagined orders. I was eager to obey orders, and found in them a great relief from the uncertainty.

Incidentally, the military analogy of obeying orders, which I am now using, was and still is widespread among those infected with this obsession. "The Church Militant" means the Christians who haven't died yet, in contrast to "The Church Triumphant," who are reigning with "God" and Christ in heaven. "Onward, Christian Soldiers, marching as to war!" We've all heard of "The Salvation Army." One of the names of "God" is "The Lord of Hosts," which means "Commander of Armies." I have since learned to be suspicious of this emphasis, preferring both freedom and responsibility for myself, over mindless obedience. But way back then clear orders were a relief, and I didn't notice that I had simply made them up.

I was sure, at age sixteen, that God wanted me to be a medical missionary. I even knew where, in an almost unknown Asian country, which soon became much better known, not as a place for missionaries but as a place for soldiers — Korea.

God's will for my life was the question. When I was young and stupid, I knew exactly what it was. It was not based in any way on the first big question, "What do you want?" It had nothing to do with, "What aptitudes do you have? What skills do you have? What interests do you have? What intentions do you have? What kind of human being are you?" It wasn't even based on the question, "What needs to be done in this world?"

The will of God was a plan imposed from the outside, by persons who were bigger, and loaded with psychological influence, onto a terrified young pip-squeak. "What is God's will for my life?" In order to end the pressure, and the dreadful uncertainty, an answer to the question was invented and pounced upon and grasped and hung onto for dear life.

But then a problem arose. Desire raised her beautiful ugly head. "What do you want, Harry?" The question had never been allowed to surface before, had never been allowed to sneak into consciousness at all. But Desire is powerful stuff, and hard to bottle. Freud admitted in one place that humans experience "somatic pressure," as he called it, in varying amounts. He admitted to experiencing only a little, which makes him seem strange to me, even now. I experienced a very great deal of somatic pressure, for which I am now thankful. I have learned to refer to this crisis in my life as, "Saved by the Glands."

I found myself in the odd position of having to talk "God" out of his will for me! What audacity! The Eternal Source of Power and Justice and Love in the Cosmos has this plan, established before the foundation of all worlds, and this little squirt is asking him to change it! Here is some evidence that people are capable of believing marvelous quantities of nonsense.

Desire, including the glands, but not limited to them, persuaded "God" to change his mind about Harry, and let him go to seminary instead of medical school and become a missionary, but not of the medical kind, and, incidentally, to get married. So, Harry latched on to this new "Will of God," and proceeded again, pell-mell, hell-for-leather, to obey the new set of orders.

It is absurd. What is the will of God? A plan? A previously determined and inexorable course of action? A general divine intention? A correct method of responding to every one of the hundreds of choices, big and little, that confront every human being more or less all the time? A notion which makes understandable and acceptable, after the fact, whatever happens? It is hardly any wonder that it is so difficult to discover the particulars of what it is. I know a lady who "lays before God" the decision as to whether to have peas or beans for supper. The concept begins to look preposterous on both the large scale and the small.

The whole philosophical discussion of free will and predestination could be dragged in here, but may not be necessary, because before we're finished, we may succeed in altering radically the idea of "God" in the phrase, "will of God." Then all that argument will be moot and really merely theoretical.

As it works out in practical questions of living, the phrase "will of God" is used by some people to persuade other people to do certain things, and not to do other things. "Obey your parents. It is the will of God."

"Become a doctor. It is the will of God."

"Gird on your sword and march and fight and slay the infidel. It is the will of God."

"Resist the urgings of your glands. It is the will of God, even though he made them."

"Do not take charge of, and change, your life. Instead, continue to obey the will of God." That means, "Obey me!" — "me" being whatever human authority is giving the orders.

If there is a God, how can anyone know his will, for the other person? Yet that is the common use of the idea. When the other person is little and susceptible, it results in pressure, manipulation and misery. It's always meddling.

When Peter asked about Jesus' plans for John, Jesus became quite blunt. "What is that to you?" Anyone who claims to know the will of God for someone else is an oppressor. He needs to be disarmed and steered clear of.

Self-deception is another matter. Certain people seem to need to indulge in it. Some persons are not yet ready to go on in life without clear plans and directions, not yet ready to tread water, not yet ready to wonder about what new unimaginable adventures life has in store for this new day, as each day dawns. They need to have it all planned and packaged in advance, and for them the will of God is a handy tool for the necessary self-deception. With the will of God firmly in place, persons can fool themselves into believing that everything is all planned and guaranteed to be O.K. — all safe and secure.

But it isn't.

C. The Fear of God

Persons who are weak and little and whose pain-receptors are functioning properly feel afraid, at least sometimes. Some are afraid of falling; others are afraid of the dark. Some are afraid of sabre-toothed tigers, or imaginary monsters; others are afraid of thunder and lightning, or deep water, or earthquake.

Some are afraid of being hit; others are afraid of blood. Some are afraid of big kids; others are afraid of adults. Some are afraid of the loss of love — this one is the root of guilt. Some are afraid of punishment. Some are afraid of failure — this one can cause complete paralysis. Some are afraid of what others will think or say — this one in the hands of oppressors replaces hitting in the assortment of tactics used to keep other persons under control.

All the phobia-words are fun to catalog. Agoraphobia is the fear of open spaces. Ochlophobia is the fear of crowds. Acrophobia is the fear of heights. The cartoon character, Charlie Brown, a fearful young fellow, was discussing these words with Linus. Linus finally found the word which described his problem. "Pantophobia."

"That's it!" shouted Charlie. The fear of everything.

Some are afraid of "God." I never saw or heard the word "theophobia," and now I wonder why. "Theophobia is the beginning of wisdom," the proverb says.

The fear of God offers great advantages to those who feel it. If indulged in seriously enough, the fear of God can liberate one from all the other fears. Fear God, the Maker and Ruler of all the powers that be, and you need not fear anything else. Fear God only.

I tried to live that way for a while, but found myself puzzled over things I observed. I wondered how persons who said they feared God could approve foreign policies based on larger and larger body counts. I wonder yet how persons who truly fear God can vote for and pay for the nuclear warheads of the world. I still wonder how persons who fear God can poison the air and the water and the soil of the only planet we have to live on.

"I tremble for my country, when I remember that God is just." Thomas Jefferson said that, thinking of slavery and foreseeing the Civil War, and thinking of his own already famous words about how all men are created equal. His own personal career as a slave-owner may have been in his mind, also.

Foreign policy, elections, ecological considerations, and that sort of thing convinced me finally that most people do not fear God. They may be trusting in some para-normal Force to protect them while the rest of the world perishes, but what kind of God would that be? It is all quite confusing. Perhaps human behavior makes no sense at all.

Yet people are afraid, of many things. At the moment the most fearful thing around is unemployment. Any folly and wickedness can find approval, if "jobs" are connected with it — the tobacco industry, the nuclear war industry, the napalm industry, the nerve gas industry. The basic

fear seems to be fear of deprivation, fear of want, fear of
hunger and nakedness, fear of not keeping up with the
neighbors economically, fear of being broke. The fear of
radiation, blast, burns, nerve gas consequences, lung
cancer — all that is less frightening than having no job.
Even the fear of illness is more financial than physical or
existential these days, which is an interesting commentary
on the type of "health-care" system we now have.

People are obviously afraid of death. The clue is that
so few will talk about it. The current low regard for the
elderly is due to the fact that we remind them of that other
set of "facts of life" — not how it begins, which is now
completely unmysterious, but how it ends. Or rather, the
simple fact that it does end. We are so afraid, we refuse
to face it.

The old verse may be in error. "The fear of the Lord
is the beginning of wisdom." It no doubt depends on what
one means by "Lord," but the beginning of wisdom is
more likely to be found in accepting the fact that one is
mortal, rather than pretending otherwise.

When a human being is afraid, what is doing the
fearing? Some fears seem to be almost physical. The
body, the nervous system itself, reacts. For example,
falling, or sensing an impending head-on crash, will cause
a gut physical reaction.

But most of our fears take a little mental processing,
and thus can be called psychological. Analysis indicates
that what is doing the fearing is one's sense of oneself,
what each one refers to as "myself," what Freud labelled
the Ego. The Ego fears annihilation, or anything that may
lead in that direction.

So, to get rid of fears, perhaps we could try, instead of the annihilation of this or that object or force in our environment, or the annihilation of the very environment itself, which the nuclear warheads and the pollution techniques now make possible if not inevitable — perhaps we could try getting by with less ego. Is that possible?

The idea of the fear of God points in that direction. If you fear God, your ego is not in charge — God is. "Are you willing to be damned to the glory of God?" A lover and fearer of God could only answer "yes" to that strange question. I mean, if you say "no," God is no longer God. Are you going to detract from the glory of God, in order to salvage your puny little ego?

Someone could propose that we try to lessen ego by increasing the fear of God, but observation indicates that it doesn't work. Leaders of religious organizations, who theoretically know God best, do not lack ego. The popes have always had plenty. So did Martin Luther and John Calvin and John Wesley. So do William Graham and Gerald Falwell and Patrick Robertson. Their loyalty and subservience to "God" do not diminish perceptibly their sense of ego.

Putting ego into perspective, without particular reference to God, seems to help most. So tiny, so fragile, so imaginary, so not really there at all. And so proud, so puffed up, so ready with excuses and complaints, so hard to please, so undependable. Comedians make hay out of how laughable ego is. "I don't get no respect."

A strange footnote about fear comes to mind. The word "reverend," used indiscriminately and incorrectly as a title for certain full-time laborers in the Lord's work, occurs

once in the Bible, in the old seventeenth century
translation, that is. It is in a Psalm, referring to God.
"Holy and reverend is his name." The Hebrew means
"dreadful, fearful, awful." New translations call it
"terrible." "Holy and terrible is his name."

But his ego-ridden full-time servants, needing a way to
distinguish themselves from plain common ordinary
Christians and mere persons, latched onto that label, for
unclear reasons. Very few of them are dreadful or fearful
or terrible. Some are comical, others pathetic, many
ineffectual.

You and I don't need a God who inspires dread, and
much less a clergyman/pastor/councillor who would do
such a thing. We need to outgrow our infantile fears, and
we need a sense of humor to put ego in its proper place.

A God which inspires terror is one to be gotten rid of.
A healthy mature human is at home in the Cosmos, not
hiding somewhere from whatever is in charge and
whatever is going on.

What are we afraid of? The dark is the shadowy side
of a solid planet. Tigers are magnificent predators. What
goes up must come down. Blood is marvelous stuff, but
not to be shed, or drunk, or feared. We're not the little
kids any more, and don't need to fear the big kids. We
have learned to love, and so the loss of love is in
perspective. Only I can define what is failure, for me.

"God," the grouchy old crab who is always spoiling all
the fun, making unreasonable demands, making live toys
and playing sadistic games with them — if that's what
we're afraid of, let's be clear. There's no such thing.

Some think of "God" as a Cosmic Bookkeeper. He's

making a list, checking it twice, going to find out who's naughty and nice. How charged with punishment the scroll! People with this kind of fear tip-toe through life, afraid to do anything at all, afraid to risk anything for fear it may not be approved by the Cosmic Rule-maker. The name of this problem is legalism, and it is the source of much misery.

The Cosmic Bookkeeper, in the minds of many, is not a metaphor for abstract Undeviating Justice. He's a foolish old man. He can be tricked, bribed, persuaded and bamboozled into making exceptions to his own rules.

Even the notion that Jesus died for our sins contains this questionable error. If our legal system allowed one person to serve another person's sentence, we'd call that unjust. To make "God" into the scorekeeper who can change the score, depending on who pays, or prays, or succumbs to the authority of this or that divine representative — that is a mockery of the idea of justice.

Many adults are troubled by a sense of "should" or "ought," even when it doesn't correspond to any clear value or goal in life. It appears to be a remnant of the old childhood fear of punishment. But for an adult the grown-up child is doing that to himself, or herself. The severe parent is now powerless or helpless, or dead. There's nobody "up there" to enforce the irrational rules. Now it can be told. You can quit fearing, when you're ready.

"Be not afraid."

D. More Godly than God

Somewhere along the line, it became widely believed that "God" could only be pleased and served by persons who were pious, sober, serious, grave, and boring. More recently the word "spiritual" has been added to the list.

This new word is tricky. "God" is supposedly a Spirit. We are partly spirit. Those who take "God" or the spiritual aspect of human nature seriously are "spiritual." But what does it refer to?

We can be warned by the inference that implies that those who are not spiritual are inferior, if not bad. The tradition is full of this, separating sheep from goats, saved from lost, blessed from damned, causing much heartache.

Dietrich Bonhoeffer, the young Lutheran pastor and theologian who was murdered by the Nazis, wrote in **Letters and Papers from Prison** that it would be a mistake for us to try to be "more godly than God." His correspondent was wondering about the rightness of marrying. Bonhoeffer wrote: "Spiritual persons often have a jaundiced view of sex, marriage, physicality, their own and other people's bodies. It is hardly any wonder. Our Hebrew/Christian tradition was begun by patriarchs who thought of women as property, and furthered by celibate priests and monks who thought of women as 'vessels of sin,' as one of them so quaintly but clearly put it. He, as a matter of fact, was denying his own Doctrine of Creation, which teaches that all that is, including bodies and sex and sexual differences and sexual pleasures, all derive from the same divine Source."

The "God" obsession can lead persons to distrust, and then dislike, their own bodies. The sensual pleasures of life become suspect, as if "God" hadn't made them and our capacity to enjoy them. Tastes, smells, feels, touches, even more than sights and sounds, are suspect for some reason. The Puritans, who helped set the tone in this country, distrusted all of it — music, theater, art, dancing, games, festive clothing and festivals generally.

"God" can make it hard to relax, to rest, to stop and do nothing, to daydream, to smell the flowers. Even when stopped, you're supposed to be busy praying and meditating, not enjoying. It's all patriarchal propaganda, obviously, if not serious mental illness. And now the documentation is in. Laughing is good for you; it releases chemicals in the brain and body, which heal. Smiling is good for you, and certainly for those you share them with. Resting is good for you. Stress is bad for you. Self-inflicted stress seems to be more damaging than that which comes from outside. And "God" is inside, not outside.

The notion that "God" won't let a person rest, or enjoy, indicates the need to get him off that person's back. If it's guilt that's bothering that person, he or she needs to get to the bottom of it, make amends, if possible, and accept the unchangeable, if that's what it is. But if it's some inherited belief that a person has been hauling around, that life is supposed to be heavy, somber, sober, serious, no fun and dull — that can be gotten rid of.

To the extent that we can relieve suffering in the world and share prosperity and happiness, you and I and all of us should be doing so. But the one suffering person you can do the most about is yourself. The one person you can change is yourself. It does not help any of the suffering millions of the world for you to keep yourself miserable. That does not improve their lot at all. It worsens the lot of those close to you who care most about you.

"God" can not only spoil sex, pleasure and fun. The obsession can poison all of life. Persons interested in "God" are supposed to be concerned about keeping track of what kind of behavior is to be permitted in bedrooms, or on Sundays, what life-styles the Ruler of the Cosmos disapproves of. They're supposed to be more interested in heaven, death and punishment after death than in life itself. It's a strange assortment of meddling and irrelevant interests. It gives a person a strange appearance — that sober, somber, pinched, up-tight, fearful, superior, easily shocked look of one who disapproves of the odor in his nostrils. Fellow-humans are being kind when they call such persons "irrelevant." They are really a colossal pain. If "God" is making them that way, they need liberation.

Healthy mortals know they are mortal, and want life to be a joy, for themselves and for others, while it lasts. Death is on the true pilgrim's shoulder all the time, and it does no harm to be aware of it. But if the attitude toward life, and death, which is inspired by "God," spoils life itself, taking all pleasure, fun and joy away, then it makes sense to seek relief, and change.

◇   ◇   ◇

E. Ogre-Father God

I snorted when I first saw one of those big black billboards that contain a brief message in white lettering, signed, "God." Then a TV morning talk show hostess noted them and thought they were a very good thing, and isn't that anonymous fundamentalist millionaire who's paying for them just wonderful! I found I had to take another look and then I thought some more about what the billboards said and what they really meant. They come from and encourage the great obsession and a restored sense of wonder could free us from that.

[1] **"Don't make me come down there!"** — **God.** I can hear the tone of voice of this one. It takes me back sixty years. Very young children, playing too rambunctiously, one crying, in the upstairs bedroom. Adults downstairs, trying to read, or listening to the radio. "Don't make me come up there!" It could be either mother or father, two different memories, two different uses of that same warning tone. So we calmed down, because if either one did come up, there would be serious trouble.

This billboard reduces adult humans to the toddler stage of life, or tries to. It also assumes the three-story cosmos, with heaven above and the earth beneath, which hasn't been anything but mythology since Copernicus. Infantile

43

humans must deal with a God who is menacing, threatening, frightening, trying to frighten, insisting on things being his way, demanding that others do what he wants. I'm thankful that there's no such God.

[2] **"I'm making a list; checking it twice."** — **God.** We know where this comes from. We suspected it all along. God is really Santa Claus, the Cosmic Bookkeeper — and his concerns are about "naughty and nice," not honest, not just, not heroic, not compassionate, not courageous. We little kids — there's that again — we're expected to do what he wants, which is "be nice," to get on the right list, so that we can "get stuff." That last bit has a very up-to-date ring to it. But who really believes in Santa Claus? Who needs to take this God seriously?

[3] **"What part of thou-shalt-not don't you understand?"** — **God.** This is a rephrasing of something I first heard from my daughter, who was dealing with her four young daughters. "What part of NO don't you understand?" The meaning was clear. "This is not a discussable matter. Argument is futile, and forbidden. I have the authority, the size and the will to enforce my way. Do what I say, or bad things will happen to you."

Again, adult humans are reduced to the role of little children. The commandments may be outmoded, peculiar to a particular patriarchal culture and irrelevant to our own time and place [graven images?]. They may be inherently unfair and arbitrary. It doesn't matter. Do what they say. Does "Thou shalt not kill" include capital punishment and war? Most fundamentalists don't think so. Does "Thou shalt not commit adultery?" include heads of state and other high officials? Forget such quibbling, and obey, the ogre-father says.

[4] **"You think it's hot here?"** — **God.** Here we have threats, serious hostility and menace, hellfire, eternal conscious torment, punishment, legalism, loopholes, escape clauses, and the requirement that one believe absurdities. And who does it frighten? Little kids. Little kids only. It becomes abuse, spiritual abuse. Kids need love, and so do we all. If this is a joke, it's not funny. If it's not a joke, it's sick.

For God to try to get us to do what he wants, to behave as he expects, he threatens to hurt us, to isolate us forever, to make us really regret it forever and ever with no hope of paying back and being done with it. What kind of God is this? What kind of people believe in this kind of God?

[5] **"We need to talk."** — **God.** At first glance this looks like the least offensive of the five examples, but it's the worst of the lot. "We need to talk." There's trouble and we need to talk about it and tend to it. Who says this? Parents whose authority is slipping. Spouses whose trust is giving way. "We need to talk."

Not me. Let me out of here. I was just leaving. I'm going far, far away. I know who's saying this. That same unforgiving, uncomprehending, thoughtless father-figure who insists that everything has to be "my way or else."

I know real fathers like that. "The kids never call." But the father does nothing but berate them when they do. Why should they call? Just to catch more hell. "We need to talk." No, thanks. Keep your threats and your list and your punishments. I grew up.

◇   ◇   ◇

E. On Meddling

A great deal of meddling is done in the name of "God." Crusaders marched long distances to kill people who didn't accept what the crusaders believed was the one single only true faith. "God wills it!" they chanted. Of course, besides slaughtering many Muslims in the so-called Holy Land, they also burned down Christian Constantinople, breaking that city's economic power, which may have been the real reason they were sent in the first place. Meddlers then and often since are really dupes of persons who don't care much at all who believes what.

The days of the crusades are not over. In recent time organized meddling by gangs of convicted mass-murderers was aided and abetted and paid for by "God"-obsessed people who believed that persons who approve of the public ownership of the means of production should not be allowed to run a country. The meddling in Nicaragua was serious, including such things as assassination, arson, mining of harbors, systematic murder of teachers and nurses, and bombing of women and children in day-care centers. The clue to understanding the Crusades of the Middle Ages applies in modern times. The powers behind such murderous meddling do not care who believes what. They simply do not want to allow the people of what they formerly regarded as a colony of theirs to begin to be in charge of their own lives.

This meddling business is very strange. When bishops and other special agents of "God" make pronouncements about the morality of modern Crusades, or nuclear war, or poverty, there is a hue and cry that they should mind their own business. They're not supposed to know anything about politics, history, war, military alliances and tactics, foreign affairs, local problems or current events. Even when they do know about these things, their opinion doesn't count. They're supposed to "stick to religion" and leave these practical matters to certified scoundrels. When a bishop says that nuclear war is a question of morality, the scoundrels accuse him of meddling in areas where he doesn't belong, like science and politics and economics.

The "God" of these persons is concerned only about a sort of morality that has little to do with ordinary human life. So when other persons who take "God" seriously begin to sound like prophets instead of priests, it will be called meddling.

"Now you've left off preaching, Harry, and gone to meddling!" It was said at the church door in a joking tone and manner, but seemed to mean that something in the sermon had struck a nerve. It reminded me of the little bell that rings when you hit the bull's eye at the shooting gallery. What had I hit? Prejudice, greed, foolishness?

But later I realized that much of what I had been doing really was meddling after all. The causes I espoused weren't bad, but some of my motivation was.

What causes this inclination to meddle? In the large movements like Crusades and contras, it is simply greed and ignorance. But sometimes, looking at smaller scale activities, the original motive is very fine. Someone has found something of great value. Release from fear, perhaps, through trusting some higher power, which they'll call "God." The relief feels so good, the person wants to share it. So he goes unasked and uninvited into the innards of someone else, offering this marvelous gift, this truth, this insight. I've heard the analogy of "one beggar telling another beggar where to find food."

But not everyone needs or wants the explanation, the relief, the "new life," that the meddler is so eager to share. Often some kind of put-down is implied, such as, "You can't figure this out for yourself." Sometimes the help simply hinders, as in the case of the Boy Scout who helped the little old lady across the street, even though she didn't want to go!

The best guidance for the well-intentioned meddler is there in his textbook. "Let your light so shine before men." If you have the secret of life, if you have experienced unconditional Love from the Source of all Power and Truth and Justice in all the Cosmos, let's see it. Let's see it operate. Don't talk about it so much. It will be wrong to shoot or bomb people because of it. Instead, do what it says. Exemplify it. Other verses come to mind. "By their fruits you shall know them."

Some people can't be helped, no matter how hard the meddler tries. No one can be helped, really, until he's ready and willing. And sometimes the helper is simply meddling, acting the role of a busybody.

I found a new scene from **Pilgrim's Progress**, that is, I made one up. Pilgrim meets Helper, coming down toward him, on the Path. Helper is very fuss-budgety, worry-worry. "Don't forget this. You'll need that. Let me give you some advice."

Pilgrim is pestered, bothered and hindered by the smothering fussiness of Helper. Finally Pilgrim asks Helper, "Why don't you go on up the Path?"

"Oh, I can't just now. I'm a helper."

"Well, let's go on up. We could go together," Pilgrim suggests.

"No, I stay down here, and help people," Helper said.

"I wonder if maybe you're delaying people," Pilgrim says.

"No, I'm helping them."

"Well, when are you going to go up the Path yourself?" Pilgrim asks.

"Oh, I'll come later," Helper says.

"You know, you're drifting down the Path in the wrong direction, and you use this helping crap as your excuse. You're not going, and you're not really helping. C'mon up. You help others most by going on up yourself!"

"No. Not yet. I'll stay here and meet the next pilgrim," Helper says.

When I was a pastor, I was assigned the official task of worrying about what other people believed. "Oh, she can't join the church; she doesn't believe Jesus is the Son of God."

"Oh, he can't be an elder; he doesn't believe in the Virgin Birth."

"Oh, we don't need to help them; they're Catholic."

Strangers moved into a new home in the neighborhood,

and I was programmed to ask myself, "I wonder if they believe in God? I wonder if they go to church?" Imagine that! Instead of the good questions, like "Are they friendly? Are they interesting? Are they happy? Are they in pain?"

For a while the group I was pastor of did a study together, called "The Church and Its Changing Ministry." I stayed in position as a clergyman a little longer than I might have, by accepting the analogy of the coach of an athletic team. The rank-and-file Christians had "the ministry" to the world. I had received the training — mostly Biblical languages, it was, which seems a little strange, thinking about it now. I mean, what did that really qualify me for? But I had that training and the task of preparing and encouraging the "ministers," who were all the people. All the people had "the work of the ministry." Ministry means simply service.

I kept jumping into the game from the sidelines and getting penalized. I was doing things like protesting the investment in fall-out shelters, and the indiscriminate shelling and bombing of Vietnamese villages, and the refusal to serve a hamburger to Americans of dark skin color. I found I had to change my idea of coach on the sidelines to player/coach, one who is in the game. I simply couldn't stay off the field.

The whole thing collapsed when I realized that I was out there alone. My team didn't want to play at all. Social action was serious body-contact sport in the sixties. They'd call it "hardball" now, and my team wanted more placid, more comfortable parlor games. I had no choice but to quit the team.

After a while I realized how much of my activity at that time was really meddling. I don't apologize for my involvement in the causes of peace and racial equality. But I understand my inner motives better. It is very hard to help people. They don't want help, really. They want oppressors off their backs. They want us to quit bombing them. They want a fair chance. They should have all that. But "help" is more often than not an expression of some kind of supposed superiority, and is quickly spotted and resented and then all the intended good effects come to nothing.

Besides, I was the one that needed help. "Leave me alone," I raged. They did, and I licked my wounds, and reviewed the situation, and pondered and studied, and finally I got "God" off my back. The irony is that that's what the church people had been paying me to do for them all along. "You do the praying, you do the studying of the Bible, you be good, you be pious and spiritual and non-physical — so that we don't have to." The pay indicated that I'd get along best, if I could become "spiritual" enough so as not to need food or gasoline.

But I wasn't much good in those days at getting "God" off other people's backs. I kept quoting Amos and Jeremiah, and disturbing folks. I called some things "salve for Christian consciences." I quoted, "Peace, peace, when there is no peace."

A strange disturbing thought comes to mind. I wonder why I am writing this book. Could it be that I am going back to all that, in order finally to get that job done, for myself? Get "God" entirely off my back, at last?

I hear a voice, telling me, "You are in charge of your

life." The voice continues: "Do not turn over the running of your life to anyone else."

I think the voice is my own best self, calling to me. "It is fine, even a good idea, to ponder in advance the principles by which you are going to run that life that has been entrusted to you. Love, fairness, honesty, reciprocal services rendered, open friendliness, retentive memory — that's what I'd recommend, but you decide," the voice says. "'Be wise as serpents, and innocent as doves.'

"No one else has as much at stake in your life as you. No one else is capable of caring as much, or doing as much, about your life as you. Your life is the only one you can do much about at all really. So do it! Change it, if necessary. Tend to your life, first and foremost. The most important piece of creative work that anyone can ever do is one's own life.

"It's time to quit meddling. Gossip is meddling. Busybody 'helping' is meddling. Helping with strings attached is meddling. Judging is meddling. 'Judge not, that ye be not judged.' Permitting oneself to be unjustly treated is allowing meddling. Permitting manipulative persons to have their way is allowing meddling.

"Let everyone be doing his own thing, busy at it, engrossed in it. Share, yes. Meddle, no."

So, I share, or try to, by writing this book. But sometimes I fear that my own sense of relief, and even excitement, over finding freedom from the great obsession is too much for others to benefit from very much. Sometimes I feel that I have found the cure for a disease that no one else has.

F. No Thinking Allowed

A key line appears in an excellent movie about *los desaparecidos* of Argentina, **The Official Story**. When the wife begins to question the husband about where their adopted daughter really came from, he says, *"¡Deja de pensar!"* "Leave off thinking!" The "God"-obsession seems to require the same thing. No thinking allowed. "I believe, because it is absurd," stated Tertullian, a leading patriarch of the early Christian church.

One of the queens in **Through the Looking Glass** bragged to Alice that she used to believe six nonsensical things before breakfast. Practical sensible Alice thought that strange, but in our time it's almost a prerequisite to getting along, not only as a queen or any other kind of powerful world leader, but as an ordinary person as well. And yet it is obviously not a good idea, to believe nonsensical things. Part of the requirement for taking "God" seriously these days is to believe large quantities of nonsensical things. I know, because I used to do it.

"Pie in the sky by and by when you die," is what many have believed will be the reward for letting someone else run their lives in the name of "God." Karl Marx called it, "The opiate of the people." To the extent that the "God"-obsession keeps oppressed people resigned and quiet and unrebellious, Marx was right. Poverty, hard work under miserable conditions without pay, slavery, waste of talent and potential — all this has been allowed and even encouraged, in the name of "God." Revolution has always been ruled out by the rulers of churches. The Pope has correctly labeled the theology of liberation, "Marxist." But just because Marx said it more than a hundred years ago, doesn't mean it can't be true. Marx got some of it from Amos, and some of all that concern about equality and fairness is in the teachings of Jesus.

Individuals, as well as oppressed classes, have allowed "God" to function in their lives like a deadening drug. If a person has remained in a bad position, continually downgrading herself and her abilities and her worth, remaining submissive because of a false modesty which was learned early on from people who wanted her to be disabled by this obsession, she now has permission to wake up. She has nothing to lose but her chains. She has been believing nonsense. Rewards to be received some other time, on some other plane of being after she dies, are a fraud. "Now is the accepted time. Now is the day of peace, health, wholeness and freedom."

Some people cling to an infantile need, and project it onto all of Reality, and call it "God." The need for a protective responsible Father, which may or may not have been adequately met in childhood, is often at the bottom of this obsession. Someone who will be in charge, someone who will have the whole world in his hands, someone who will keep track of everything, including you and me and all our problems, that great Daddy in the Sky — it is an illusion, and not worthy of our allegiance. We need courage, honesty, energy, time to get our wits about us, resolve, persistence, good will, understanding from other living human beings — but not a Heavenly Father.

Rituals

The rituals which have come down, by which we supposedly connect ourselves to "God," are nonsensical, also. Christianity has become irrelevant, in the minds of so many thoughtful persons of good will and honesty, because it requires so much participation in nonsense.

Consider baptism, for instance. At first it was a symbolic washing. Then it became a symbolic drowning, dying and rising to newness of life. It made sense then, and still could perhaps, if that was what it meant. But ages ago the ceremony was changed. The water became holy, and specially consecrated men were required to handle it, as if the water were a magic substance, as if it were dangerous, almost as if it were radioactive. People were taught to believe that persons who came in contact with this water were safe. All others were doomed and damned eternally. Now, is that nonsense, or isn't it?

For a while the nonsense included the notion that sins committed after baptism could not be forgiven. The Emperor Constantine, the one who made Christianity legal and then exclusive in the Roman Empire, delayed receiving baptism until he was on his deathbed, and pretty far along at that, for fear of committing a sin afterward that couldn't be forgiven. Later that very notion was decreed a heresy and belief in the magical properties of the water itself was highlighted, along with the notion of the absolute hopelessness of anyone unbaptized ever finding eternal happiness. Limbo had to be invented as a place to put obviously "good" pagans, like Plato and Aristotle, and even Old Testament heroes like Moses and Elijah, who weren't ever baptized. Limbo is a sector of hell, don't forget, but with a minimum of torment.

In my younger days, I never accepted the arguments for infant baptism, even as a clergyman. It seemed to me that it was obviously superstition, and nonsense. I did try for a while to let baptism be the symbolic bath and symbolic drowning. Colleagues used to argue with me over my refusal to baptize my own infant children, but I argued back and now I see how telling that argument was. "I don't believe in the kind of God who would punish eternally an innocent child, just because her Daddy is stubborn and in error."

Later that argument came to be put more strongly and became a crucial agent for dissolving in me this obsession. "What kind of God would do such a thing to an innocent child? Who cares about such a God? If such a God exists, I reject him. I oppose him, in the name of love and good sense. I am not interested in him."

Another nonsensical ritual is the communion, so called. It began as a symbolic meal and a time to remember, and made perfect sense. In a loving, sharing family, every meal is a time of thankfulness and mutual respect and listening and laughing and good feeling. At such times we remember those who are absent.

But look at the unintelligible magic ritual that the communion meal has become. The elements have been changed, once again made as if radioactive. Only certain supercharged officials dare be in charge of them. The withholding of the cup from common ordinary people in the Roman Catholic Church told all about the evils of clericalism. "We can't let ordinary Christians have the full benefit of this magic stuff. We must keep it for ourselves, and thus make sure that we're always superior." Only those who believe in a sort of nonsensical magic could accept such arrogance.

For centuries the churches have tried to manipulate people's lives by the threat of depriving them of this magic food, or forbidding their sharing it. That makes the ritual an expression of meanness, rather than support and sustenance. To pretend that "God" enters a human life through a specially blessed wafer, and not through every crust of bread and swig of water, makes "God" a small and private matter, a commodity on the market that some company can pretend to have a corner on, something far less than the Source of all Life and Power and Meaning in the Cosmos.

If the churches could change the elements used in the ritual, they could perhaps salvage something. Cake and ice cream. Chile and beans. Sauerkraut and mashed potatoes. Pizza and beer. But they won't do that. Instead they argue about wine or grape juice. In the meantime the joy of shared meals doesn't need a symbol. They can be what they really are, each time. No nonsensical belief is required at all.

There is another ritual that required adherents to believe in nonsense. Ordination is the ceremony by which those persons who can handle the other rituals are designated. Certain persons are set aside from common ordinary people, and only they are allowed to baptize or serve the Holy Supper. At first glance, ordination seems to be providing helpers for "God," human agents for his activities in the world. But in practice, the ritual limits "God." He can only work through these special ones. Arguments about the requirements for the office are still going on — which gender or genders are allowed? How much education is required? Does homosexuality have anything to do with it? What sort of study counts as preparation? But the ceremony of ordination itself is what supposedly makes it work. Gender and training are preliminary requirements.

My own experience with all this led me finally to conclude that it is all a fraud. The people thought I had been changed, but I knew I had not. They thought I had special powers, but I knew I did not. They thought of me as a sort of stand-in for God, which was ridiculous. People threw cigarettes in the stove as I approached, as if they thought I represented God's disapproval. They seemed to think that if they fooled me, they had fooled God. Sermons on the all-seeing eye of God did not help clear this up. And even this mortal representative of God was harder to fool than they thought, evidently.

People waited for me to come and pray for the sick or the dying, as if my prayers were more efficacious than theirs! Why did they think that? Isn't it obvious nonsense? The Quakers figured this out, and refused to ordain a class of clergy at all. Each one could seek the guidance of the Inner Light as effectively as any other. In fact, I have come to believe that each one must do exactly that, that no outsider can possibly find the correct guidance for someone else. Each one must do it, in secret, for himself, or herself.

Whenever someone claims to be the representative of God on earth, or "the vicar of Christ on earth," or any such thing, he is asking the world to believe in nonsense. It is alarming how many millions still believe it.

◇ ◇ ◇

My God

Some years ago, when Haiti was under the control of the purest kind of dictatorship, the Ambassador of Haiti to the United States of America came on the TV news and used the phrase, "My President." It sounded strange in our ears.

Even in our flawed democracy, no one tries to say, "My President." We don't say, "My Governor," or, "My Mayor." We say simply, "the President," "the Governor," "the Mayor." There's just one of each, for everybody.

"My Congressman" could mean the one, among the many, who represents me. I'm displeased with "my" Congressman a good bit of the time, voting as she so often does for things I disapprove of. And nowadays, of course, "my Congressman" could indeed mean, "the Congressman I bought and paid for." I can't use the phrase that way, since I'm not buying.

Is anyone, except an insane megalomaniac, saying "my Universe"? The National Geographic Society published a book some years ago, called **Our Universe.** It was a bad title. The Universe isn't ours. The Universe is not American. If they meant, "the universe we are in," it is still a bad title. There is only one of them. We are all in it. "Universes" is a contradiction in terms, as if we could imagine the plural of "everything." Such straining only messes up the language.

We know an elderly lady in a nursing home who uses a similarly strange phrase, "My God." What does "my God" mean?

Mostly it is an expletive which means simply, "I have been startled," or "I have just been surprised," or "I am astonished and can't keep quiet."

Nevertheless the attachment of the possessive pronoun adjective, "my," to a deity is a strange thing to think about. In what sense can a human claim to own a god?

Perhaps the phrase could mean that this particular god is the one I worship, among all the others. The prophet Elijah's name means exactly that. "My God is Yahweh." Elijah is the prophet who had the great contest with the rival gods, called Baals, on Mt. Carmel. "The fire of YHWH fell" on Elijah's altar, whereas "no one answered, no one heeded" the pleadings of the priests of Baal.

We don't think our elderly friend was using the phrase to express her allegiance to "God" instead of other deities. If you asked her, she would almost certainly say that there is only one God. Yet she, and many monotheists, persist in using the phrase, "My God." She really does refer to the One in charge of the entire world. He has sent a sickness to her, she believes, and there is no cure that will work. Yet she refers to that Source as "My God." It is a puzzle. If there is only one God for everybody, how can he be hers, or mine, or anybody's?

What does "my God" mean, on the lips of professed

monotheists? Can a human own a deity? Can a human be the proprietor of the Source of Power and Justice and Love in the Cosmos? C. S. Lewis noticed how strange the possessive case is in our language. We can say, "My wife," and "My country," and "My boots," and the meaning is not always exactly the same. The meaning of "My God," is still far from clear.

When this writer graduated from a theological seminary decades ago, they gave him a degree called, "Master of Divinity." He has never gotten over it. Master of Divinity! "I say to one, 'Go,' and he goes. And to another, 'Come,' and he comes. And to another, 'Do this,' and he does it." "My god!" It's crazy!

As a phrase, "our God" is hardly any better than "my God." It expresses division, superiority, hostility, and leads to war and violence. Ancient and recent history reeks of the blood spilt in the name of "our God." Politicians of every sort call on "our God" to justify everything from genocide to mutual assured destruction. "God" becomes part of our top-secret arsenal.

The world will be better off when we all give up such irrational code words for the meanness inside us. "My God" and "our God" are the excuses we use to hide our own unkind attitudes and misdeeds. Perhaps we can grow past the need for such unhelpful phrases.

Creator

The idea of creation comes up right at the beginning of humanity's thinking about "God." "In the beginning God created the heavens and the earth." The Biblical record begins with two different partially contradictory accounts of this.

"God" is already there before anything has been created. Then he makes things. In one story he brings them into being by speaking, "by the Word." They exist at his say-so, one could surmise. In the other older story, God forms things out of stuff, mud, the dust of the earth, quite like a ceramicist forms things out of amorphous clay. The creator begins with an amorphous mass, called Chaos, and then forms or calls into being an orderly Cosmos. The concept is extremely anthropomorphic. That is, the story-teller is describing "God" as if he were a kind of glorified human being, a potter who can breathe life into the forms he has made, who can force his world into an orderly pattern.

There are many problems caused by this doctrine of creation. It states that the world is an artifact, something that a Maker made. Creationism as a philosophical position is full of difficulties. The Creator cannot be located. The Creator is consistently referred to as "He," which is obviously wrong, unless we accept a kind of innate inferiority for femaleness. To say that the Creator is a spirit, and thus cannot be located and has no gender, doesn't answer anything; it just brings up a new set of unanswerable questions, like, "What is a spirit?" and "How can spirit affect matter?" A great deal of energy has been wasted on these wrongly-put questions, without producing any really satisfying answers.

Creation sets up the notion of incarnation. If "God" made the world, he can't know exactly what it's like to be the world, or be some part of it, so he has to "come" and be born and find out by being part of it. It's as if a carpenter had to become a chair he himself had made, in order to understand chair-ness fully. Word games and paradoxes and contradictions fill up the minds and the books of those who have to try to reconcile all this. We need a God with skin on, they say, a God who can suffer, a God who knows our creaturely limitations, who knows what it's like to exist for a while and then experience non-existence, by dying. So we have the Creator trying to be a creature, so that he can communicate with us.

"He's still workin' on me," chirps a happy-sounding popular gospel song. It continues with the old image of the potter and the clay. The singing sounds a little too facile and too glib. That same image of the potter and clay made Jeremiah the Prophet uneasy, when he used it. The potter wasn't pleased with what his pots were up to, he says. The angry potter shattered some pots that were fired already, and smushed down into a fresh shapeless lump others that were still unfired and soft. Some people feel that some sort of Creator is doing exactly that to their lives.

If there really is a Creator/Lord, then empires are in trouble, including ours. He disapproves of exploitation and violence, the prophets say. Ecclesiastical organizations are in trouble, too, for blatant disobedience, clearly.

All these theological/philosophical problems go away if we discard the notion of a creator. The wise child's question, "Who made God?" is the correct one, perfectly logical, not impudent, and not at all unanswerable. No one made the Creator. The "God" who makes things, or who

made all things, is a myth, a metaphor, which itself was
made up by humans long ago. And it is no longer a very
helpful myth. Our ecological troubles today are caused,
partly, by the story that God made the world and then
gave it, as disposable property, to humans, who, in turn,
are destroying it.

There is an alternative to the idea of creation. School
boards are squabbling over it all over the country just
now, and the issue is "evolution." I like to call the
alternative concept Monism. All of what there is is One
Thing, not two. The Whole Thing is more like an
organism than a machine. Monism implies that What-
There-Is is alive, since part of it, namely this planet at the
least, is alive. Monism implies that What-There-Is is
intelligent, since various levels and types of intelligence
show up in many places, right here on this tiny planet. We
see it in the arrangement of particles in atomic nuclei, in
the assorted DNA molecules, in an ant hill, in dolphins,
in libraries. We could wish for more of it in this planet's
centers of government and corporate industry.

The Cosmos grows, from inside itself. It changes and
develops and builds and discards and preserves and
expands and contracts. "Evolution" is a word for all that.
It may even blink on and off at times. The Cosmos
expresses itself in a myriad of ways. You are one of them.

Try this train of thought. Instead of thinking of yourself
as an artifact that "God" made, a tool, an animated toy, a
slave, whatever — imagine yourself as one of the many
attempts of The All to express itself. Your being and your
experiences are utterly unique. You can teach "IT" things.
"IT" has never done this before, that is, what IT's doing

right now in and through you. IT has never experienced this quite this way. IT is learning, at this moment, by being you. The more aware of all this you are, the more IT learns. Consciousness, an awareness that goes beyond sensory impressions, seems to be mostly what IT is up to, in the case of humans like you. So let IT be up to a lot of that. Pay attention. Be aware, now.

Being aware that you are a unique expression of IT will make you resistant to that mistreatment to which our civilization is subjecting us. By means of homogenized and falsified information input, along with all the drugs, legal and illegal, combined with the computerized quantification and categorization of us all, we are in serious danger of becoming completely impotent, identical, replaceable machine parts. Some of us more cantankerous types resist that, because we know that we aren't that.

We don't need creationism to be unique. We do need to become fully aware of who and what we are. Bringing in a creator makes it less lonely, perhaps, and maybe a little easier to talk about superficially, but it is a myth with no factual basis.

Each one of us is IT, doing ITS thing, struggling to be conscious and sensitive. You may let that Creator/God bogeyman go, and feel free to be yourself, an expression of The All. And, when you run into a metaphor, or a myth, don't forget that that's what it is.

Savior

Many God-obsessed people hold to the idea of creation and the notion of God as Savior, both at the same time, even though they turn out to be contradictory, when examined carefully.

The idea that a Savior is needed implies that something is the matter with that which God created. To say "Man spoiled it all by sinning," doesn't account for it, if you believe in creation, because God created man. This is an old insoluble philosophical/theological problem, caused by trying to hang on to two contradictory positions.

It turns out we don't need either position. One part of What-There-Is did not create another part. It all just simply is. Likewise, one part doesn't need to save another part. In fact, it would be unjust, or immoral, if the penal-substitution theory of salvation were true. That's the notion that an innocent party, Jesus, took the rap for the guilty, that is, all the rest of us.

The Savior business slips into injustice early on. Jesus supposedly died to save those who believe in him, but becoming a believer is a tricky and chancy business. Whole civilizations have been excluded. Reasonable, sensible, sensitive persons, like you and me, are in danger. God saves some and condemns others, for unclear reasons. Calvin the Theologian pushed God into some marvelously unjust corners, in his arguments for the sovereignty of God. In effect he asserted that God can do whatever he pleases, and save whomever he likes, and doesn't have to answer to man or to man's paltry and faulty sense of justice.

So we have all the divisions in the world, in the name of God. The saved and the lost. The sheep and the goats. The blessed and the damned. The washed and the unwashed. The circumcised and the uncircumcised. The ins and the outs. The white and the black.

What's at the bottom of this savior business? The Messiah was going to save the Jews from their Roman oppressors, according to the ancient hopes of the people. Instead, according to the teaching, Jesus saves his followers from their sins, and in so doing saves the creation itself from corruption. The political content was taken out, that business about the occupying Romans, even though Jesus was hanged according to the story, for claiming to be the King of the Jews, and some sort of perceived threat to the Empire.

The history of the mystery religion movement may be helpful at this point. The world was regarded as evil, corrupt and doomed. The dead and resurrected Savior-God will save his followers from the hopelessly damned world. It's a wonder this new religion could interest any Jews at all, since they generally had such a strong belief that the only God there was had made an essentially good world. But bad circumstances allow persons to believe strange things. God will save his people, the hope declared. The new religion relocated the problem, not in political/ social/economic troubles, like persecution and war and taxation, but in "sin," some internal personal fault, that the Savior could cure.

I first ran into the savior thing as a very little boy, in a reading book called, **First Steps for Little Feet**. A child was inside a burning building, and a man rushed in and grabbed him and carried him out running, and saved him. The man was the child's savior. Then the analogy was drawn. My sins were like the house afire, and Jesus saves me from them. Actually, my sins as a little boy didn't amount to much at all, and then later when they did begin to, at the onset of puberty, if that's what they meant by sin, and so it seemed, Jesus did not save me from them. He couldn't put that fire out.

And I'm not sure the rescue notion is a good one to put into the head of a sensitive person anyway. If there's something the matter with me, with the way I think, the way I understand things, the way I instinctively react to things, the way I really am at bottom, then I do not need some outsider barging in to rescue me. I need to get my mind to work, and my resolve, and my courage. I need to get busy and pay my bills and change my ways and rethink my values and re-order my priorities and clearly define my goals and get off my bottom and do something.

Some of Jesus' sayings put this very plainly. "Make friends with your adversary quickly, or you will never get out until you have paid the last penny." Each one must pay his own debt. Forgiveness won't change that. Nobody is going to take any one's place. Each one must correct her own life. Each one must live with consequences. Each one is the one who must take responsibility for that life. People want Jesus to take the rap, to go their bail, while they remain drifters and chronically lost. People want a Hero to come and rescue them and make everything all right and get them off the hook and take over their lives.

There's a paralyzed man at the pool of Bethesda. Jesus asks him, "Do you want to be healed?"

Right away the guy bursts out whimpering, "I have nobody to put me into the pool when the water is disturbed. Somebody always beats me to it." The myth is that an angel comes down and disturbs the water from time to time and the first one in after that is healed. "Nobody will help me. I need a Savior. Somebody always elbows in ahead of me." The text doesn't say so exactly, but Jesus must have been extremely indignant.

JESUS: "Get up!"

PARALYTIC: "I can't get up. I'm paralyzed. That's what paralysis is! That's the definition. Paralytic!"

J: "Get up!"

P: "I can't!" [Whimper and wail]

J: "Get off your bottom!"

P: "O.K. O.K."

J: "Now, pick up that pallet."

P: "I can't! I'm paralyzed! Remember?"

J: "Pick it up!"

P: "O.K. O.K." [Mutter, mutter, mumble] "Jesus."

J: "Now, get out of here."

P: "How?"

J: "Walk!"

P: "Walk? I can't walk. I'm paralyzed!"

J: "Don't give me that. Get going!"

P: "O.K. O.K. I'm going. I was just leaving."

That's the best savior story in The Book. "Rise, take up your bed and walk." And be rid of your self-pitying paralyzing disability.

Some of that old story badly needs retelling. "Are you he who is to come, or shall we look for another?" disappointed Messiah-seekers ask Jesus on another occasion. Jesus doesn't really answer those disillusioned Savior-hunters. "The blind see, the deaf hear, the lame walk, the poor have good news told to them. Make whatever you want to out of it."

I wish he'd been more blunt. I suspect he was, but the ecclesiasticators got hold of the story before we did. He didn't see himself as Savior. He had work to do. Suffering humanity is all around him in need, and these savior-seekers plague him and hinder him. Here they come with those damned rattles. "Don't ask me to save you!" he should have said. "Get at that project yourselves, if you need saving. Get to work. Begin yesterday. Get off my back!" he should have said.

◇   ◇   ◇

Theology

There's an academic department called "theology," the study of God, — the logic of God! It's the age-old attempt to make religious beliefs and practices appear rational. "The queen of the sciences," they have wanted to call it, since the days of Thomas Aquinas. I know about this because I studied it. I left it all because it became clear to me that it doesn't make sense, that it is not at all logical, and that attempts to make it seem so are fraudulent. Religion is whimsy and mythology, and that would not be all bad, if true believers were not being encouraged, even required, to believe that it is literally truth and fact.

Fundamentalism insists that myth and metaphor be taken literally, such things as the six days of creation, and "no man cometh unto the Father but by me," which excludes all but a comparative few. At the same time fundamentalists tend to distrust most theologians, because the theologians bend hard sayings — at least some of them do some of the time — in order to attempt to preserve logic and remain in good academic and "scientific" standing.

Some of the topics that theologians have argued about are quite remarkable. Abortion is evil, some say, because a human life is being ended. Maybe there's a logic there, but most medical scientists don't accept it. At any rate the true motivation behind all the nasty anti-abortion behavior was revealed during the bombardment of Iraq some years ago. "Abortionists have killed 180,000 of our future soldiers." Abortion destroys the expendable cannon fodder ahead of time. There is a horrible mean streak at the bottom of this view. It is the height of cynicism to call it "Pro-Life."

Theologians have argued about clerical celibacy. Some think the priests who can perform the miracles of baptism and transubstantiation, which changes wine into blood, must be unwed. They assert that this denial will not necessarily interfere with healthy human sexuality in spite of centuries of logic and evidence to the contrary. To pretend that the celibacy argument is not machismo and patriarchy continuing the age-old attack on sexuality and on women is illogical. To call these arguments "theology" forces thoughtful people to conclude that "the logic of God" is not logical at all.

Theology has been used to support racism and slavery also, but the worst, and most illogical, use of theology has been in the defense of state-sponsored violence — what we

call war. This was the issue that drove me and my on-
going ability to think clearly out of the game of theology
altogether. I took part in discussions in which fellow-
theologians argued in favor of bombing little children and
defoliating entire forests, as well of building up an arsenal
of many thousands of nuclear weapons, whose only
function was to unleash huge quantities of blast and
radiation. They did this in the name of "God," and even
Jesus, the so-called Prince of Peace.

It had gone beyond logic. I could imagine, just barely,
a person stating with sincerity, "I believe because it is
absurd," as Tertullian did so long ago. But those pro-war
arguments did me in. If that's "God," I'm leaving. It isn't
logic — I was sure of that and still am.

Dim-Witted God

For years I kept an ever-expanding file, labeled, "It's
a Good Thing God Is Stupid." My wife hated it. I called
it the working title of a book I'd sit down to write some
day. "It'll never sell," she warned, "because people don't
want to be reminded that they are stupid."

I thought she was making something of a jump there,
but then I realized she was correct. As soon as it was
pointed out to them, as my book would do, that they
believed that the Source of Truth and Justice in the entire
Cosmos is essentially stupid, people would quickly hop
from that idea to demanding, "Hey, who you calling
stupid? God? Or me?"

The project languished for years, but observations of

instances in which people indicate that they think they can fool God or trick God kept piling up. Now it's time to share them, in this manifesto which is recommending that we declare our independence from such a God. Here where I live we could call this God, *Dios Pendejo,* but that verges on the nasty.

"Be not deceived. God is not mocked. Whatsoever a man sows, that shall he also reap."

But sincere believers in God mock him all the time, believing he is easily hoodwinked, easily fooled, quickly and easily deceived. We can observe true believers living their lives as if the All-seeing Eye of God couldn't perceive all the lies and deceptions.

People believe, judging by their actions, that God is confined to shrines and temples and churches, and that he has no interest in what we do out here in the "real world." People believe he can be persuaded to change the rules, to change his mind, to condemn the innocent and forgive the guilty.

People, including his official representatives, teach that God is satisfied with one-tenth, or less, far, far less in most cases. They think he'll take one day and leave the other six, or that he'll take one hour and leave the rest of the week.

The sections on sacrificial offerings in Leviticus are not quite as boring as they appear at first glance. It takes some perseverance to plow through it all, but offerings are worth pondering. The "whole burnt offering" is something one can comprehend easily. In God's honor, in order to show one's obedience and submission to God, the worshipper offers an animal, or a sheaf of grain, or a loaf of bread, and the priest places it on the altar and simply burns it up, while God and the worshipper watch. But worship doesn't have to be so drastic, such a final letting-go of what is offered.

There is also the "wave offering," in which the priest takes the offering and in the midst of all his prayers waves it in front of God at the altar there. The belief is that God accepts that, and then the worshipper can take his gift back home and eat it. It appears that God is allowing himself to be fooled, that the intention is good enough.

A friend of ours suffered a heart attack, serious enough that family members were summoned from far away. A retired family-friend rabbi also came. His suggestion was that they change the sick man's name. That way they could "deceive the angel of Death," who supposedly had the length of the man's life written somewhere on a scroll. Our friend survived the ordeal, but our view of the inscrutable, inexorable sovereign God suffered somewhat. It seemed that they were successful in fooling him.

Many worshippers behave as though God were willing to treat them as exempt from the rules. "Let me off the hook. Excuse me from the consequences of my own actions." These are variations on an older theme. "I'm different. I'm special. I can get away with it. Lying will solve it. No one will ever know. Secrets are safe."

When I taught fifth grade boys, I observed something which comes to mind at this point. Some of the boys, not all, behaved as if they thought the teacher was very slow-witted. The pencil flying through the air "fell," or even "jumped," as if the teacher couldn't see clearly, as if he couldn't make correct inferences, as if he could be sweet-talked and grinned out of comprehending just what was going on.

Some parishioners did the same thing. I mentioned already the lady, visiting in the home where I was about to make a pastoral call. She threw her freshly-lit cigarette into the kitchen range, as I approached the back door. She thought God disapproved of her smoking, and believed she could fool God by fooling me. I've pondered it much, since then. If God is stupider than I am, and really is running the world at the same time, then the Cosmos is in trouble. I saw her throw the cigarette. Did she think God didn't? Now that I no longer believe that God is there at all, I marvel at the almost all-pervasive notion held by those who do believe, that the Force governing the Whole Thing is essentially stupid, easily fooled, successfully lied to and bamboozled, capable of showing partiality and favoritism.

People try to give God information — it's astonishing what is said in some "pastoral prayers" during public worship. People aren't quite sure about God's wisdom or compassion. A distraught young woman was interviewed on TV, after giving away the body parts of her recently deceased infant. "We just hope God understands."

Whatever happened to the sovereignty of God? Doesn't God know everything? Isn't everything that happens his doing? That belief can cause hard philosophical problems, very old and insoluble ones, to be sure, but I must say that that old Sovereign God was preferable to this Dim-Witted God.

When God's representatives change their definitions of what is sin and what isn't, they make it hard for God. Is eating meat on Friday a sin, or isn't it? Is cremating a human body a sin, or isn't it? Who defines what sin is? God? Someone who isn't God? Who, then? And what's this talk about "infallible"?

If I ran the world, slavery would be a sin, but many of God's representatives have said that he approves of slavery. In these very dangerous times, we're having great difficulty weaning humanity from war, partly because God is described by so many as being in favor of it, or not really opposed to it much.

Well, God may be something other than stupid. He may not be there at all. "Cry aloud!" Elijah taunted the priests of Baal, at that great test on Mount Carmel, during the time of Queen Jezebel. "Perhaps he is asleep and must be awakened. Perhaps he has turned aside," Elijah teased.

Turned aside? What does that mean? "Turned aside" happens to be the translators' euphemism for "stop and take a leak." Really! Like any man-made idol, like any man — Baal, or Dim-Witted God, has to urinate from time to time, can't come to the phone just now, can't deal with what needs dealing with. "Cry aloud!" Maybe we can rouse him, or disturb him. "But there was no voice. No one heeded. No one answered." He isn't there.

Some very thoughtful and aware and sensitive people have concluded that God isn't there at all. It does no good to attack and dismiss those people, calling them "atheists," as if that were a horrible condemnation and the end of the investigation.

Besides, by inference we can observe other atheists, who are not thoughtful or sensitive. They claim to be restoring righteousness, upholding and enhancing morally upright behavior and values, "family values," they like to call them, while they lie and cheat about election fraud, and agitate in favor of war and capital punishment. They drag God's name in the mud, making other people ashamed of the God these phonies prate and sing about.

It's a good thing God is stupid. If God wasn't stupid, he would deal with those liars, who claim to believe in him and speak for him. But I do not believe those fundamentalist preacher/politicians believe in God at all. They are play-acting. They are trying to get people to believe things that they themselves know are not true.

How could Pat Robertson believe that there is an eternal God of impartial Justice and Truth, who likes him better than he likes other people? It is impossible that he could believe that. It is not a believable proposition. It is pure nonsense, and he knows it. He could, perhaps, if he wanted to, believe in nonsense — it's been done before, but he cannot believe in God. Not really. He would be paralyzed in terror and immediately expire. He, in fact, knows perfectly well, or at least is betting his life and his business and the future of his "eternal soul" on the fact that there is no God at all. He is an atheist and a hypocrite and a liar. He says things that he knows are not true and cannot possibly be true. Meanwhile, he wants us to believe in Dim-Witted God.

II. Some History

A. The History of "God"

The natural uncomplicated religious attitude of human beings, and also the oldest and most primitive, is called "animism." It goes back to Neanderthal man. The Cro-Magnon, who made the cave paintings at Altamira almost 30,000 years ago, also were animists. Animism is still practiced in the Amazon Basin, in New Guinea, in the Kalahari Desert and in the Australian outback.

The history of "God" must begin here. Animism is the belief that all the universe is alive. The rocks, the mountains, as well as the trees, the grasses, the animals, the soil, the rivers, the lakes, the ocean, the clouds, the sun, the moon, all the stars, our tools, the materials we make our houses out of — it is all alive and sentient. It is all "animated." A spirit lives in every thing.

Animism can develop in many directions. By the time Christian missionaries and European anthropologists arrived in some places a nasty negativism had permeated this belief system . The world and all its contents were regarded as hostile. The animating spirits were thought of as demons or devils, enemies of man. They needed to be placated or deceived by means of horrifying rituals and taboos. The missionaries believed that the cosmic terror they encountered in the minds of those animists justified their own work of obliterating those beliefs. They were ruthless in stamping them out.

But animism need not be negative. Perhaps the Europeans were "projecting" some of their own fears onto the "natives." Actually the basic idea behind animism makes a kind of ecological sense. Humans are part of a living web of interconnections. There have been many successful and benign adaptations to the local ecology, such as that of the bushmen of the Kalahari Desert, who have survived in ways we don't fully comprehend. Unfortunately they and their way of life are being exterminated by the relentless spread of Western Civilization, with its web-destroying combination of "economic interests" and the God-obsession.

In other situations animism underwent development, long ago, before the invention of cities or writing. Joseph Campbell describes this process in the first of his four-volume work, **The Masks of God**. The cultural evolution beyond simple animism went in two directions, depending on the livelihood of the human group involved.

Hunters concentrated on the animal spirits. They saw themselves related to those spirits, descended from them somehow. Their main concern was to secure permission from the spirits to use the bodies of the animals they hunted and killed, and to guarantee that the spirits would continue to provide more animal bodies for their use. The totem-spirits were then enlisted to help with the hunt itself. The humans sensed their relatedness to the animals.

Human groups who "advanced" to farming had other worries, like the weather and soil preparation. A major concern came from the observation that the seed had to die in order to sprout and multiply. Ritualistic means of guaranteeing that dying and multiplying process were invented, with sacrifice at the root of the belief system. Sometimes there was a symbolic dying, but often real slaughters took place as part of the ceremonies. Victims were selected in various ways: captives, virgins, first-born sons, chief's sons, and others.

At this stage of religious development the humans called the animating spirits they had to deal with gods and goddesses. There was the deer god, the corn goddess, the sun god, the rain god, the river goddess. To guarantee the continuation of their way of life, people had to deal with all these gods. This stage is called polytheism.

Most persons in our culture have learned about "God" from the Hebrew/Christian religious tradition. The Bible contains much of that lore. The historical sections of the Bible begin at the time of Abraham, and we can pick up this history of God there.

Abraham's urban family were polytheists. Abraham became a deviant, reverted to herding, and decided to practice monolatry. That meant that he was going to worship one God only. The god's name was YHWH. Later that name became so supercharged with magic, no one would pronounce it. They substituted instead, "LORD," meaning "owner, master." The root of YHWH is the Hebrew verb "to be," and means "He who is," or "I AM what I am," or even "What there is." The name is unpronounceable. "Jehovah" uses the consonants of YHWH and the vowels of the Hebrew word for "LORD," [Adonai]. Some scholars, quite certain that "Jehovah" was not the original pronunciation, use "Yahweh."

YHWH became the tribal god of the extended family of Abraham. YHWH took care of the nomad flocks, the pastures and the wells, the fertility of ewes and women, taboos about diet and menstrual blood and sexual behavior, and laws about slavery and inheritance. Social control, within the tribe, was a religious matter, and still is in many parts of the world. Most of the people reading this book probably experienced a modern form of tribal control through religion at an earlier stage of life.

Every tribe had its own gods. The Abrahamites also had theirs, but only one. They didn't deny the existence of the gods of the other tribes, with their different names and different taboos and commandments. They ignored them, or scorned them, out of loyalty to YHWH. In fact, YHWH admitted to being jealous, and according to the priests and prophets, became nasty whenever any of his people tried worshipping other gods.

The descendants of Abraham's grandson, Israel, seem to have invented the idea that YHWH became involved in human history. At least they take credit for it. Not only hunting and agriculture, but historical developments are also YHWH's concerns, they said.

The most drastic and alarming historical activity, up to that point, had been war and conquest. So YHWH became a war god. He brought his people out of Egypt, defeated the Egyptian pursuers, whipped the Amalekites and others, fought for and with his people in the conquest of Canaan, and promised to drive out the Canaanites, the Hittites, the Hivites, the Perrizites, the Girgashites, the Amorites and the Jebusites.

But the Israelites did not complete these genocidal mopping up operations, supposedly because of their fascination with those other gods. YHWH did not drive the foreigners out of Canaan, but left them there to "test" Israel. The twelve tribes lived in something like anarchy for a while. "In those days there was no king in Israel, and every man did what was right in his own eyes."

That fatal interest in the gods of the Canaanites can be accounted for. The nomad Israelites were herdsmen, and plunderers. The Canaanites were farmers. The technology of farming included the worship of the Baals, the localized fertility gods. Their worship included human sacrifice, but also some rather sexy behavior, which no doubt helped arouse the interest of the newcomers. Besides, hunters who are going to learn how to grow grain need all the technological assistance they can get. They couldn't resist the temptation to check out the temple prostitution business, and the local ceremonies "on every high hill and under every green tree."

The judges and the prophets of the Israelites raged against this corruption of YHWH-worship. Yet in the end, YHWH had to become versatile enough to be a fertility god himself. How else would the grain grow for the Israelites?

Meanwhile YHWH helped get a central government organized, choosing Saul as king, then rejecting him in favor of David. YHWH's exploits as a war god helped put together a large empire, for David and his son, Solomon. Then YHWH permitted the splitting away of most of the empire from Solomon's son, Rehoboam, leaving two nations, with one god, YHWH.

The larger non-Davidic nation, called Israel, was swallowed up by Assyria a couple of centuries later. This development was accounted for by saying that YHWH gave up the struggle to win them away from idolatry. They became the "ten lost tribes," but they weren't lost in the sense that they could turn up later in Great Britain or Utah, as some have claimed. They were lost in the sense that they were deported to Assyria and absorbed into the population there and exterminated as a separately identifiable people.

Meanwhile, YHWH as a jealous war god, was in trouble. All he had left was a tiny state, called Judah, named for the larger of the two tribes that were left. It consisted of little more than Jerusalem and its rocky suburbs, under constant threat from both Assyria and Egypt. It was not much for a war god to be proud of. Judah was finally overwhelmed by Nebuchadnezzar, king of the Mesopotamian Empire of Babylon. The Jews, as they were called by then, went into exile.

This was a very important crisis, for YHWH. The world almost lost him, at this point. But some strange notions were invented, and saved him. Some of the earlier prophets had laid down important groundwork, and the prophets of the Exile completed the task.

YHWH was active in history all right, they taught, but not as a divine secret war weapon of the Jews. YHWH became identified with certain abstract ideals, like Truth and Justice. Because of injustice, not religious jealousy, YHWH could change sides, and fight on the side of Nebuchadnezzar against his own people in Jerusalem, to punish them and teach them. The prophets Amos, Hosea

and Jeremiah said this most clearly. Second Isaiah and
Ezekiel clarified it further, while in exile.

YHWH is invisible. He cannot be depicted, or named.
YHWH cares more about social justice, kindness, mercy
and truthfulness than the temple and its priests or rituals.
He arranged to have his own temple destroyed to prove it.

Now in exile in Babylon the Jews discover that
YHWH isn't confined to the land of Canaan. He is not
merely a local tribal war god. YHWH is present in
Babylon, too, the prophets believed and taught. YHWH is
even present over there, in Persia. Their new king, Cyrus,
has been put into position by YHWH, in order to arrange
for the Jews' return home later.

YHWH is everywhere. YHWH made everything, and
rules over it. YHWH is the only god there is. He is the
Creator of all things, the heavens and the earth. The
whole earth is his, the world and they that dwell therein.
He loves all people. He chose the Jews to be his special
suffering servant people, to be the agents and channels of
his intent to bless the whole world.

This is monotheism. There is only one God. The Jews
know who he is. They know his name, YHWH, but it
cannot be pronounced. By this time he also goes by the
generic name, "God," [El or Elohim] and will use that
label henceforth. He is a supporter of justice, because he
is just. He can be stern, but he dislikes indiscriminate
violence. He chose the Jews, say the prophets, for reasons
that are inexplicable, to be instruments of his purpose to
do good to all. He is not anyone's secret weapon against
the rest. No people are his favorites, but he has special
tasks for the Jews.

Well, so far, so good. We have one invisible God, and a chosen, but not favorite people. We also have a world full of violence and misery, especially where the large empires abound and interact.

A couple of centuries go by characterized by violent imperial musical chairs: first Babylon, then Persia, then Greece, then Rome. For sensitive and aware people it seems hopeless. The Jews are kept going with a strange hope for a God-sent Deliverer/Messiah, who many are sure will have an anti-imperial political/military mission.

Among the other peoples of that time and place — especially the Greeks, the Persians, the Syrians, the Egyptians and the Romans — thoughtful and sensitive persons give up on the world in large numbers. Mystery religions arise in every sector, all very similar. The general description of them all will sound very familiar.

A young god/hero, born of a virgin, lives an exemplary and miracle-filled but short human life, and dies unjustly. He rises again from the dead, and lets his followers in on the secret of eternal life, beyond death. He becomes their savior, from sin and physical limitations. As the world goes to final total ruin, he rescues his followers and joins them to himself in eternal other-worldly bliss. For some the savior's name was Attis; for others it was Mithra, and there were others.

All of these new movements were an expression of cultural malaise and decadence, which scholars call, "The Failure of Nerve." The world was regarded as unsalvageable, and not worth saving. Individuals were satisfied with saving their souls, and the mystery religions grew by promising that kind of salvation.

In the early decades of the Roman Empire, another mystery religion arises in the Near East, and spreads to Greece and Rome. This new one builds on that history of "God" that we have been tracing from Abraham. A Jewish prophet/rabbi, Jesus of Nazareth, is lynched with tacit but illegal Roman approval. He is declared Messiah, Son of God, and resurrected Savior. Worship is offered to him.

Most Jews regard that as a step backward. The One invisible God cannot have a Son; he is not that kind of fertility god. Besides YHWH has not turned his back permanently on the world he has created, Jews believed. But the Christians interpret the suffering servant passages in Isaiah's writings to refer to Jesus, the Savior, not to Israel as a people. The blessing God has for the whole world is the news that the God/Savior of the Christians will save them, too, if they submit to him.

For several centuries it was not certain which of several of these popular and very similar mystery religions would win the day. The Roman Emperor Constantine, in the 4th Century, made sure that it was the God of the Christians to whom all the world must some day submit. That prepared the scene for missionaries and fresh new empires, and popes who can lock people they don't like out of Heaven. It led to Inquisitions and Crusades and unbelievable slaughter in the name of Peace and Love. It made possible Christian rulers capable of believing that they are God's chosen instruments for the punishment and destruction of whole peoples, and now recently of the very planet itself, if need be. All in the name of God.

B. Questioning God

For many centuries thinking about God was placed in the hands of specialists and left there. They were called theologians, and non-theologians were not supposed to think about the big questions, such as, "Is there a God?" or "What is God like?" The rank and file were simply expected to obey.

Theologians came and went, and over the ages schools of them could be identified, based partly on the accidents of history and partly on the contents of the books the theologians wrote. "Oh, that's Augustinian." "Oh, that's Thomistic," for Thomas Aquinas. "Oh, that's Calvinism."

Thomas, in the 13th century, attempted the great feat of summarizing all there was to know about God, including logical proofs of his existence and detailed statements as to his nature and purpose. He built a great theological system, which still stands as authoritative for Roman Catholics, and is quite impressive. John Calvin, in the 16th century, built a similar system for the Protestant Reformation.

"Systematic Theology" is still the name of the most prestigious department in seminaries, and it consists of three main branches: "The Doctrine of God and Creation," "The Doctrine of Christ and the Atonement," and "The Doctrine of the Church."

But what is Systematic Theology? Is God a system? Can God be put into a logical system and kept there? Many of the questions Systematic Theology deals with seem very far removed from the life most people are living, and sometimes the logical and theological answers verge on the absurd or the immoral.

For example, one theologian has stated that, based on his theological premises, it was possible for Adolf Eichman to go to heaven, if only he would accept Jesus Christ as his personal Lord and Savior in time, before the Israelis hanged him, but that it was not possible for any of the six million Jews whose murder Eichman supervised to do so, since they were Jews, and therefore not believers in Jesus Christ. They were dead and therefore it was too late for them to change their minds by converting. That kind of thinking is simply repulsive. In addition, I think we have a right to question the relevance of such exaggerated concern about "going to heaven."

People have real problems to deal with: floundering marriages, alcoholism, petty gossip, hunger, birth, funerals for sixteen-year-olds, pestilence, war, despair. Systematic Theology often makes assertions that have little or nothing to do with anything important.

But some theologians started a process which could be called "questioning God." Many of them have been labeled "heretics" by the official churches that had made them into experts on God matters. In more recent times philosophers who never pretended to be Christian at all have analyzed God rather carefully. Friedreich Nietzsche and Bertrand Russell come immediately to mind. And some who were Christians and not heretics at all also advanced the process. Their observations will be of interest to any who want to break free of the God-obsession. Let's look at a few, just in our century, briefly. **Karl Barth** wrote his 20th century version of Systematic Theology, and made some startling assertions, such as, "Christianity is not a religion." What could he mean? It certainly looks like a religion. When you read Barth carefully, you can spot his awareness that sociologists have studied the religions of mankind and noted those two main functions: (1) grant divine sanction for whatever the social group is doing, and (2) placate the numinous, which means, as we have already said, "to get those mysterious and unseen powers off our backs."

Barth doesn't think that Christianity is doing that. Other religions do that, but Christianity is not a religion. It is Truth, he says, final revelation from God about everything. Barth also referred to "the God who really is God," as if to say that when some people use the word "God," they are not referring to the "real God," that is, the one that Barth is referring to.

Rudolph Bultmann asked Barth to state his preconceptions. Barth was puzzled. "I have none. I'm just telling you how it is." The scene verges on the comical. No human being can function at all without his own perspective and preconceived notions, but Barth couldn't spot his own, and denied having any.

Bultmann, it turns out, was questioning "God." He admitted that he was ready and willing, and even eager, to bring Christianity into line with modern scientific thought by tossing out every instance of what he called "interventionist myth." A lot is stripped away, however, when that is done.

Imagine that the world is like a toy ant farm. God is the boy who owns the ant farm. The ants go about their business, doing their thing, marching two by two, digging tunnels, eating, laying eggs, all that. The boy, from time to time, reaches in and pokes the ant farm with a stick, breaking up tunnels, disturbing eggs, crushing individual ants. He interferes with life in the ant farm.

Bultmann says that's not a good metaphor for God and human activities. He means that God does not, or maybe cannot, interfere like that. The story of the parting of the Red Sea to save the Israelites, for example, is a case of interventionist myth. Bill Cosby summarized the idea perfectly decades ago in his comedy routine on Noah, when Noah brought in two female hippopotomae. To avoid the trouble of having to go hunt for a male, Noah asked God to change one of them. God replied, in Cosby's version of the story, "You know I don't work like that." Bultmann would have approved of Cosby's way of telling it.

This idea of removing interventionist myth makes good sense. Can God interfere, for whatever reason? Is there such a God? But if God doesn't or can't interfere, big chunks of the Bible and tradition have to be let go.

I recall my own train of thought, when I began questioning God. It had to do with the word "supernatural." I was writing plays, and my teachers made clear that "deus ex machina" was a cheap trick used by lazy or dishonest playwrights. There's no such thing in real life — a God outside of the machine, "machine" meaning the world and all its interrelated activity. When the playwright has let his story become so complicated, so insoluble, so unrealistic, that he can't bring the pieces together in the last act except by hauling in some kind of Rescuer from the Outside, he needs to "think about it some more," as those writing teachers often told us.

I came to apply the writing lesson to my thinking about The Whole Thing. There is nothing "supernatural" anywhere. If something exists, it's natural. If it isn't natural, it doesn't exist, except in imagination. There is no Entity that made the world but isn't part of the world, that can come in from outside and interfere, suspending the rules of Reality on a whim. I agreed with Bultmann about "interventionist myth."

Dietrich Bonhoeffer, who has been cited earlier, wrote non-systematic theology from his cell in a Nazi prison. He lamented the fact that we think of God as a stop-gap, mainly. Whenever we're stuck, we bring God in. Otherwise we don't need him or bother with him much. As the circle of our knowledge widens, we push God further and further away, out on the outer rim of an ever-enlarging circle, more and more distant, less and less relevant to our daily lives. For the most part, Bonhoeffer noted, we can get along without God. He seemed to be regretting that. The fact that he was writing from a Nazi death row prison no doubt influenced his thinking.

Paul Tillich coined a phrase to describe God — "The Ground of our Being." His thought was widely rejected by those who bothered to try to understand it. They called it "oriental," which it is. It was called, "Pantheistic," which it also is, in a way. The Ground of our Being was too big a mental jump for most Christians, including Tillich's fellow-theologians.

Nothing less than the existence of God was at stake in this proposition. It was an old question. "Does God exist?" "Exist" means "to be outside." "To be," but in the sense of "to be, as over against something else." But God, Tillich said, is the Source of all existence. Things exists because of God, one could say, because God is the Ground of existence. But God, as an entity separate from other entities, does not exist. It would have been a bombshell, if it had been allowed to go off, but most folks heard only another dud. "Theologians don't make sense," concluded the vast majority of those who ever heard of this idea. Most people never heard of it at all.

But it does make perfect sense. If God exists, outside of this existence that we are in, where is he? Where can he be found? And if he's not in this same plane with us, how can he have any influence on what happens here? "Truly, thou art a God that hidest thyself," lamented one of the old prophets in a bad moment.

Bishop James Robinson came along in the 1960's with a book called, **Honest to God**. Bishops aren't supposed to admit that they doubt or question the formulae of systematic theology, but this one did. He did his doubting in print, and then asserted flatly that there was no God "up there." The old Biblical and medieval three-story universe of Heaven, Earth, and Hell, isn't there. There's no such thing. But the bishop went on. In our Copernican universe, with the earth spinning in an orbit around the sun, there is no God "out there," either. Where is he, then? Where shall we look?

Look "down here," Robinson said. Look "in there."

Within yourself, and in the human connections you find yourself in the middle of. He was trying to understand Tillich's idea of the Ground of our Being, but it leads inevitably to pantheism, orientalism, alchemy and heresy. The questioning of God is still going on. Another bishop has turned up, this time in New Jersey, **John Spong**, who writes that Christianity must change or die. **Robert Funk** in his book, **Honest to Jesus**, continues the attempt to discern what Jesus of Nazareth really taught and did, apart from the mystery-religion stories which couch the evidence. Remythologization proceeds apace through a scholarly organization called The Sea of Faith, based in Britain. **Don Cupitt**'s book, **Taking Leave of God**, demolishes the "God" of theism. These scholars want to redefine "God" and "religion," while continuing to use both terms.

Where is God? What kind of God exists? Where do the important things come from, things like life, love, faith, justice, longing, hope? Are they dreams that die at dawn? Is there any Ground, any Basis, for them? Why should we cast our lot with them? Is there nothing to do and nothing to hope for, nothing but a quick grab at more than one's share, something as evanescent as the mist, before it's all gone?

We need to be aware of "anthropomorphism." We humans have fashioned God in our own image. Probably we couldn't help it, being human. In the Bible, especially in the early sections, God is extremely humanoid. He takes afternoon strolls in the Garden of Eden in the cool of the day. He has hands, and fingers, and feet, and a footstool, and a face. Moses got to see his backside, it says. God has feelings, like anger and jealousy and grief and vengefulness.

Here we are, trying to think of the Source of Cosmic Being, the Original Void, the Unmade Uncaused Cause, the Root of Power, Justice and Love in all the galaxies — and we're stuck with images that suggest little more than a glorified human being! Perhaps we can't help it. Maybe we have to do that. But at least we could admit that we are doing it! God is really a figure of speech, for all those ideas of Source and Uncaused Cause. Every attribute that we assign to "that" is our own doing. Reality is surely something else.

Whenever serious questioning is going on, there will be some who are determined to fend off the questions and prevent the discussion from going where it's tending to go. These hinderers have a trick up their sleeve — they'll announce, "It's a paradox!" A paradox is a pair of statements which contradict each other, both of which must be regarded as true. The word is derived from Greek — *para* [beside] and *doxe* [teaching]. Parallel contrary ideas are held in position in the mind at the same time.

With reference to God, the paradox is seen when he is described as both Transcendent and Immanent. Here are the two mutually contradictory statements:

[1] "God" is Transcendent, Sovereign, Inscrutable, Wholly Other, not to be questioned or doubted or disobeyed.

[2] "God" is Immanent, Within, Hidden up close, Closer than breathing.

The trick is the insistence that both have to be taken as true, even though they are contradictory. The same

Entity cannot be Wholly Other and Wholly Intimate, at the same time. This particular paradox can be taken care of by deciding which of the two proposed statements is true and discarding the other. "You must decide," the still, small voice says.

I personally have come down favoring the second statement, taken as metaphor, and I now regard the first statement as simply false. I do not think a Wholly Other Entity is there at all. There is no Entity that Made and Rules over What There Is. That notion comes from thoughts and feelings about a patriarchal royal potentate, projected onto the Cosmos.

Whoever is reading this book, this far into it, is doing so because at some level, to some degree, you have allowed yourself to become a theologian and question God. You have your own reasons, based on your own experiences. They are excellent and valid reasons, unique and precious experiences. It may encourage you to know that you aren't the first person of good will to question God. It can be stated flatly that your questioning is a sure sign of your inner good health.

C. The Most Popular Idol

The dictionary defines "idol" thus:

[1] an image of a god, used as an object or instrument of worship,

[2] in monotheistic belief, any heathen deity,

[3] any object of ardent or excessive devotion or admiration.

The Hebrew prophets railed against idolatry, using the first two definitions. They called the idols of neighboring nations, "the work of men's hands." Sculpture, engraving and painting suffered for centuries in their tradition, because of the perceived danger of idolatry.

But the notion is more important when taken figuratively as in the third definition above. Then "idol" doesn't mean art; it means what humans care most about.

Nineteen hundred years ago, the most popular idol was called ROMA. Later it was called HISPANIA in one area and FRANCIA in another and BRITTANIA in yet another. In the name of that imperial idol, great quantities of murder and enslavement and arson and theft took place. All of that was excused with explanations of "civilizing responsibilities," and "the white man's burden," and "the spread of the message of the Prince of Peace and his salvation."

. In our day and place this same most popular idol

could be called AMERICA, but our arrogance has carried us on beyond such obvious nationalistic idolatry. We have deceived ourselves as a result. Our idol is called simply "God." That generic term makes it so simple, so slick, yet so hard for some folks to spot.

Many people assume that God is an American. Some go so far as to believe, and even say, that God is a Republican, but we'll leave partisan discussions to one side. But God is indeed an American, according to this widespread idolatry. He has his priests and prophets, too, for "God and country."

God is a major participant in our national Holy Days. Proud smug prayers accentuate the celebration of Independence Day. God helped found this country in the wilderness, we're told. The people who were already here, with their established civilizations, didn't count, except as part of the fauna. They were wild beasts that had to be exterminated along with their towns and granaries. Treaties with them did not require truthfulness in word or intent. This same cynicism carries over into current uses of assassination, double agents, deception and diplomacy, all necessary aspects of the conflicts this God-obsessed nation keeps getting into.

The establishment of a fair number of the colonies was a religious enterprise. Massachusetts was for the Pilgrims and the Puritans, Rhode Island for the Dissenters, Pennsylvania for the Quakers, Maryland for the Roman Catholics. When it came time to amalgamate the colonies, all the religious disagreement was swallowed up in the new American idolatry. They separated church and state, and a large number were more loyal to the state than that vague abstraction the churches talked about.

Thanksgiving Day was set aside to offer thanks for the special protection the deity gives, not to humanity, or to Planet Earth, but to the newly arrived land-grabbing white Europeans.

Memorial Day is to commemorate the war dead, to justify the bloody history of the nation, and to fine-tune the mindset needed for future wars.

Armistice Day was originally observed to note the end of the war to end wars, but it ceased to ring true, what with Franco and Tojo and Hitler. Ike called the Second World War a Crusade, but ending war itself was no longer the goal. Since then we've had the Cold War and Korea and Vietnam and Nicaragua and El Salvador and Panama and Iraq and Serbia. So, Armistice Day has been converted into a confusing group of Holy Days, all called Veterans Day, when we honor the soldiers! Not the end of war, but the perpetuation of it, and an obscene war budget to go with it. Is anyone fooled by the word "defense"?

The American war god is named God. It's a brilliant trick. If he were called Mars or Ares or Northrup or Bechtel or something like that, this clarification would not be necessary. Even Mother's Day is part of the idolatry, because it honors American mothers only. Otherwise we'd hear more about the mothers of the *desaparecidos* all over Latin America, the mothers of famine and AIDS in Africa, the mothers of Cambodia and Vietnam and Poland and Palestine and Nicaragua.

All this can be correctly labelled idolatry, because the God is limited to a part, and does not deal with the whole thing. Any time the deity is the god of some portion, a form of partiality results, and that's idolatry.

The worship of the American war god flies in the face of all the implications of monotheism. If there is only one God, he can't be "ours." He can't be anybody's. If there's only one, he alone has to be enough for everybody. He has to be the God of the Poles, the Nicaraguans, the Ethiopians, the Mohicans, the Aztecs, the Chinese, the "communists" (whether they believe in him or not!), the Iranians and the Afghanis (no matter how fanatical their beliefs are!) He has to be there, the same for everybody. How many Gods are there? One, or more than one?

Lincoln saw a problem at the time of our Civil War. People on both sides prayed to God for victory. Was there a northern God and a southern God? What was the one single God, for both, supposed to do? Lincoln, like the old Hebrew prophets before him, turned to abstract justice for his explanation. "The Almighty has his own purposes. ...Fondly do we hope, fervently do we pray, that this mighty scourge of war may speedily pass away. Yet, if God wills that it continue until all the wealth piled by the bondman's two-hundred and fifty years of unrequited toil shall be sunk, and until every drop of blood drawn with the lash shall be paid by another drawn with the sword, as was said three thousand years ago, so still it must be said, that the judgments of the Lord are true and righteous altogether."

Partisans of American military nationalism don't think like that, and don't like that sort of public speech. They think America is first and best, and they assume that God thinks so, too. Precisely that indicates the idolatry. They think of the planet as something America can take, by purchase, or conquest, or "cultural influence." They hate it when people thwart us in any way, as has been done in Cuba, Vietnam, Iran, Panama, Chile, Nicaragua, Lebanon and Libya.

Nationalism is a very dangerous plague which infects this whole planet and needs to be eradicated. God will probably not be much help, because the word, at least for the time being, has been captured by those who think in terms of parts only, not the whole. Americans aren't the only offenders, just the most powerful. The French nationalists no doubt think that God is French.

One god for the whole planet might be a good idea, for now. Intergalactic communication will necessitate further growth in the evolution of the concept, later. For the time being, it would be a huge leap forward, or an arduous uphill task, just to bring people to think in terms of one human species on one endangered planet. And there are some of us who don't want the whales left out!

Maybe there's a way to overcome the God-obsession itself. It's surely worth a try, just to be rid of this stupid, expensive and dangerous nationalism which is currently connected with it.

D. God Is Dead

Back in the 1960's there was a brief theological flash-in-the-pan which was called the God-Is-Dead movement. James Altizer, William Hamilton and Gabriel Vahanian did most of the writing. Standard-brand theologians correctly predicted at the time that it would be short-lived. Where can you go, as a theologian, after you have announced that God is dead? As we used to say, kidding one another, "What will the preacher do, when the devil is saved?" This was a similar, although directly opposite proposition. God is dead? Now what? The whole question reminds me, for some reason, of the cartoon of the distraught-looking late middle-aged man, putting his shirt back on in the doctor's consulting room, while the doctor chirps, "Don't worry! After you've given up wine and women, you won't feel like singing anyway!"

It's easy to poke fun, but yet the movement was important, and an awareness of it could still be helpful for persons trying to be rid of the God-obsession.

The God-is-dead theology had several roots, and several branches. In one sense it was a modern revival of an old heresy. God died, they said. The Son of God, the Second Person of the Trinity, Jesus of Nazareth, died a horrible death at the hands of a squad of Roman soldiers in about the year 29 A.D. near Jerusalem. He didn't merely faint, and later recover. He died, of shock, exposure, internal injuries and a spear wound in the side.

Some medieval theologians, obsessed with death and with Jesus' divine nature, stated flatly, "God died." Other theologians wouldn't allow it, logical as it was from its own premises. Jesus is God and Jesus died, but God did not die, they insisted. If he had, the universe would have fallen apart, between Friday and Sunday. The orthodox theologians preferred another paradox, or another instance of believing a nonsensical thing. It was better than questioning the deity of Jesus or the oneness of God. But they could not allow that God had died. Those who asserted that he did die were guilty of heresy.

The God-is-dead theology of the 1960's revived that old heresy. God needed to experience human life, all of it. That's why he incarnated himself in Jesus. God needed to experience death, which is a part of human life. So he did. It sounds like a word game to me now, hair-splitting, tip-toeing around explosive contradictions, making points too fine for most people, but the orthodox theologians insisted on an important difference between saying, "God experienced death," and simply, "God died." The God-is-dead movement of the 1960's neglected that difference and slipped into what almost everyone else called a heresy and a dead-end.

The God-is-dead theologians wanted to be thoroughly modern. Like Bultmann, they rejected "interventionist myth." Like Freud, they were ready to assert that the projection of that Great Father Figure in the Sky, threatening and/or protecting, was an illusion with no future. Like Marx, they were ready to assert that the exploiters of the poor and weak used God to drug their victims into accepting their fate, their poverty and their misery. Like Nietzsche, from whom they took the phrase, "God is dead," they believed that the deity's function, for the most part, had been to thwart human creativity, making slaves and automata out of persons who never ever tested their own inherent powers.

The God-is-dead theologians made some other strange assertions. The God they spoke of was not the Sovereign Master of the Cosmos that Calvin wrote about. This one was weak and vulnerable. He was not the God of History and Justice and Recompense and Retribution, not the Cosmic Bookkeeper, not the Consuming Fire, not the Source of Power, and not the Over-arching Will.

They asserted that he was a God of Love. Of course, the Bible and many theologians affirmed that, too, but it was always a secondary emphasis. One of the key lines in the writings of William Hamilton was this: "The faith is flawed. The love is not." By "faith," I think he meant "conformity to orthodox creedal positions." He was aware that he didn't believe in what other theologians meant by "God." But he insisted that the love was still intact.

Yet the very assertion, "God is dead," emphasizes the weakness, the suffering, the helplessness, the fragility, of that love. Love can be betrayed, rejected, scorned, spurned, mocked, injured and killed. And so, from the frustratingly weak position that sensitive people found themselves in in the mid-1960's, what with assassinations and napalm and anti-personnel bombs that our taxes paid for and unconstitutional wars and tear gas and church bombings and police horses trampling people and billy-clubs and jails, it seemed that love could die. And God is love. So, they asserted, God died.

Once again it feels like mostly word games and bad syllogisms, now. But they said it, and enough people heard it to make it a "movement." God is dead. It was like giving up on Love, and on long-range Justice. Perhaps it was another instance of The Failure of Nerve. It was making the word "God" mean something it had never meant before. God, by definition, it seemed to some of us then, could not die, literally. Figuratively, maybe, but then it turns into more word games. What died? Something other than what Barth called "the real God," maybe. But these men are talking and writing as if we should be attending a funeral — God's funeral.

At that time I took the God-is-dead theology to mean something else, and so did some of them, I think. Something indeed had died, for me. Something let me down. I had put myself out on a limb, for my beliefs. At least that's what I thought at the time. But then I found nobody there. Nothing there at all. A void. No answer. No help. No support. No net. No nothing.

It was all part of how let down I felt by the so-called people of God. The church, it says in the Bible, is the body of Christ — supportive, helpful, faithful, dependable. I found that it was not so. I discovered that the church was a gathering of selfish, confused, frightened, narrow-minded human beings, including me. It was simply a group of human beings, and no more. There was no God holding it together. An enlightening cartoon of the period expressed well my new discovery. "God may not be dead, but he sure doesn't want to get involved." But I was too involved. As I extricated myself, I concluded that, for me at least, God was gone. There was no God in the picture, no God at all.

But mostly, even at the time, I saw that the truth in the God-is-dead theology was that they had identified an idol, even under his generic name, "God," and proclaimed his death, meaning his unreality. God, that God, never was, at all. God is dead. The God of the American armies and navies and air force was dead. The God of the undefeated (until then) imperialist aggressive American military power was dead.

The God of violent mass destruction at home and abroad was dead. He finally ran out of gas, just as the gods of the Assyrian Empire of Sennacherib did. Likewise the gods of the Babylonian Empire of Nebuchadnezzar, and the Persian Empire of Xerxes, and the Greek Empire of Alexander, and the Roman Empire of Caligula, and the French Empire of Napoleon, and the Nazi Empire of Hitler, and the British Empire of Churchill. They all thrive for a little while, and then they die, gods and all. The God of all that is dead. Humanity, once again, can breathe a sigh of relief. That was a God we don't need. If he isn't dead, he ought to be. For me, deep inside here, he is dead as a doornail.

The fearsome oriental potentate, that priests and people must placate with tithes and sacrifices and offerings, is dead. The God who uses fear and guilt to control and manipulate and make miserable is dead.

The projected father-figure, the great Daddy-O in the sky, who claims to know best but doesn't, the celestial Santa Claus, who is the ground of our sentimental optimism or our unfeeling fatalism, is dead. And it's good riddance.

The God who is the cosmic excuse for what we do, personally or socially or internationally, is dead. The God in whose name the majority tyrannize or the minority terrorize, the God who takes sides in our paltry selfish narrow little fights and squabbles — that God is dead.

The God who is our authoritarian problem solver, our escape from the world and the consequences of the decisions we make, especially the ones we make by default because of our laziness and cowardice and greed — that God is dead. We can no longer console ourselves with the old phrase, "It is the will of God," or even, "May God's will be done."

Someone else will have to take responsibility for such things as our undeclared wars and the suffering they cause, the pollution that is killing life forms, the cancer from the smoking, the slaughter by the drunken drivers, the dying of hope in the poor and the old and the weak and the young. We can't blame God for those things any more. That God is dead. And if anyone is going to do anything serious about any of those things, it will have to be we ourselves finally taking responsibility for our lives and the life of the planet.

But this process can lead still further. Is there a God at all? Many a careful honest thinker has concluded that there isn't. God-obsessed people, or rather formerly God-obsessed people, must face this question squarely. And it will be a mistake to become too glib and hurried with a negative reply, either, saying, "It's all crap." Let's really look at it.

Notice a trend, over the eons, reducing the number of deities. Uncounted thousands, in animism. Many, many, in polytheism. The trend was to amalgamate, and reduce the number, by arranging them in hierarchies. Finally there was a pantheon, that is, a limited number, and then a triumvirate. At last, we get to monotheism, reducing the total number to one. We need to note that very few humans can handle the universalist, one-world implications of monotheism. Most are still caught in the nationalistic, tribal idolatry.

But can this reduction be taken one step further? From one to none? On beyond monotheism. Do we need the one God, to justify or object to what we're doing? Does just and loving behavior require some kind of divine support? Must good deeds be done only "in the name of" a higher power? Can't we just simply do them?

And let's be twenty-first century empiricists, looking at what is really there, at what we have observed in our own lives and at what "scientists" report. I don't mean those mad inventors of war materials, but rather the experimenters and observers of atomic particles and genes and ecosystems and galaxies. What can we confidently believe about the unseen, about the meaning of it all, about the purpose of our lives?

I, for one, cannot flatly say that it means nothing, or that it obligates me in no way, being what it is. But what is God? Voltaire said that if there was no God, we'd have to invent him. What for? What is the use of the word, or the concept? What reality is there behind the notion?

◇   ◇   ◇

III. Breaking Free

A. Nature and Monism

The Cosmos is a remarkable arrangement. I was going to write, "a remarkable thing," but it isn't "a thing." It is everything. It is Reality. It is What-There-Is-As-It-Is.

Persons who examine it carefully always come away with a sense of wonder. Those who study how large it is bring us facts which are somehow comforting. The light from the nearest galaxy, which we can see by looking in the right direction, left there two million years ago, before there were any humans here at all. Out of every two billion photons that leave the sun, our Day Star, five reach Planet Earth. The rest go off in some other direction. I find that amazing and somehow encouraging.

Astronomy makes me feel little, and strengthens me at the same time. The Whole Thing will not be permanently ruined by our stupidity and malice. Our nastiness is contained, by order, by magnitude, by distance, by time. For that I am deeply grateful.

Persons who study the infinitely small also report facts that produce wonder, and are comforting. Particle physicists are sounding more and more like poets and philosophers. The world is less "solid" than we've been thinking, it turns out. The distinction between mass and energy is fuzzy. The characteristics of both waves and particles seem to be valid descriptions of matter/energy, even though they're contradictory. At the particle level, uncertainty is a basic principle. Heisenberg's famous summary is that you can ascertain the momentum of an electron or its position, but not both at the same time. The upshot is that this seemingly solid world is mostly empty space, mostly nothing at all.

The most disconcerting news, and the most exciting at the same time, is the discovery of "virtual particles." Electrons, it seems, blink in and out of existence, all the while. Now you see them, now you don't. The statistics about huge numbers of them hold firm, but the "existence" of any particular particle comes and goes. The ancient Hindus said that about whole worlds, too, that they blink on and off, manifest and non-manifest, Being and Non-being. For some reason the whole idea makes a body feel like dancing.

Persons who study life, which is the one characteristic of this particular planet which seems to make it very unusual, all come away with a sense of wonder. At the level of the very small, among molecules and genes and chromosomes, it all seems to be tied up with "information." Life is what it is, because "messages" are communicated, by genes, by the arrangement of molecules in strings, in spirals. It is all "intelligent" down at that level. And, that being so, the Cosmos can hardly be labeled "meaningless."

At the other end of the scale of life, persons who study ecosystems likewise share a sense of wonder. The complex inter-connections, the capacity for co-operation as well as exploitation, the incidental beauty that results so often, all the different kinds of "intelligence," as in a beehive or in a rotting log or inside the digestive tract of a man or in the brain of a dolphin — it is all indeed marvelous. The pending destruction of it all, because of industrialized and militarized human activity, seems a shame, to put it mildly.

Nature is quite marvelous, what we can perceive of it, and stirs in us a sense of wonder. But nature is larger than our perception. Our senses perceive only a narrow strip of the total range of what is. For example, we see light, ranging from deep red at one end of the spectrum to deep purple at the other. Beyond one end of what we can see, we now know that infra-red exists. And beyond the other end is ultra-violet. Plenty exists out beyond what we can perceive, it turns out. "Invisible" no longer means "not for real, not there, imaginary." It now means "beyond the range that our eyes can perceive."

Likewise "inaudible" now simply means beyond the range of what we can hear. Low frequency, high frequency — we can't hear that. But the vibrations are there. Dogs can hear things we can't, and so can dolphins. It is quite a wonder.

If our senses could be changed, sharpened, or a whole new one added, we would perceive things which we cannot now perceive and have no inkling of. Those things are there. They do exist now. We simply have no idea what they are. They seem unreal and insubstantial when we try to imagine them. They seem not to be there, but they are, lots of them. We simply cannot yet perceive them, or imagine them, or visualize them. Reality far exceeds our personal, and collective, perceptions. It is beyond all our imagining. And that can be a cause of wonder, for thoughtful persons.

We have sharpened our senses, with tools and logic, and we now do see cells and hear galaxies, and we do now believe in the existence of molecules and quasars. Nature is marvelous, more so than we often take time to appreciate fully. I find I can have a lively sense of wonder without God. I sense wonder more often now than I did when I let God run my life. A friend and colleague, way back then, tried to share her sense of wonder with me, looking at a sunset, and then at the veins in a fallen leaf, and then at the veins on the back of her hand, but I was too locked into theology to "get it." "God made all that," I said, and dismissed it, and missed the chance to appreciate all that, and her.

My life at that time, it seems to me now, was mostly abstract theological rules, fear, distrust of my body and other people's, distrust of physicality itself, and most importantly fear of truth and discovery. I was lucky, to find my way out of that labyrinth.

But I did finally set aside those childish things, and let my innate sense of wonder function freely. As I studied the myths of the world, trying to put those old beliefs of mine into some kind of perspective, I stumbled on a way of thinking about it all which may be helpful to other seekers. For what it's worth, I'll share it. I have mentioned it already. Its name is Monism.

Contrast it, first of all, with monotheism. Monotheism says there is only one god, not many. Monism says there is only one, of anything. That is, there is only One Thing.

"There is One." "What-There-Is is One." "All of What-There-Is is One." All the multiplicity we see and feel around us is made up of interacting interlocking parts, which make up One.

There is only one Universe, and in no sense is it "ours." It is bigger than we thought, including all alternate realities, everything that is on both sides of all black holes and big bangs, all imaginary worlds, all that is and has been and will be ever. And it is all One.

The Whole Thing, The All, The Sum-total of Everything make up One.

There are not two "everythings."

If the word "God" is to have any valid use at all, it will have to be as a metaphorical way of referring to that Oneness, the Whole Thing. The myths of the world, including the Hebrew myths of YHWH and "God," are all attempting to do exactly that, that is enable us to talk about THAT. Some metaphors work better than others. If "God" could mean a symbol for The All, a metaphorical monosyllabic shorthand reference to "All-of-It," to What-There-Is-the-Way-It-Is, perhaps we could continue to use the word.

Personally, though, I find the word "God" no longer very useful. It is too easy, too glib, too quick to say without the appropriate quantities of wonder reverberating, too jam-packed with erroneous and nonsensical and mean-hearted content. I find myself personally relieved to be rid of it. It continues in our language, in our figures of speech, in our expletives, but no longer in this seeker's carefully thought-out belief system.

No god at all. Just a remarkable world, and an awe-inspiring opportunity to be alive and share another day with all these other marvelous organisms. I think we benefit more, learn more, if we do without the quick and easy would-be answers and explanations which the word "God" allows. They are all non-answers and non-explanations, anyway.

There are certain kinds of situations, and certain trains of thought, which can be called "mythological." "I'm in the middle of an archetypal situation!" one may occasionally exclaim. Life has a way of making us think about it. The sense of wonder enables us to practice, when we're not in archetypal situations. When you lose your hair, or a tooth or several or all of them or your hearing, you're forced to think about it. When your crop fails, or your business, or your marriage, you're forced to think about it. When a companion dies, or a parent, or a child, you have to think about it. When you or someone you love develops cancer, or runs away from home, or is a victim of rape, you're forced to think about it.

Life seems less forceful when good things happen to us. The negative signals get more attention. A good marriage, recovery from illness, paying off the mortgage, a bumper crop, a promotion, a birth, an inheritance — these could also be opportunities to get into a pensive state of mind.

When you remember that looking at the stars is looking back in time, when you try to imagine what your life will be like ten years from now or one hundred years from now, when your grandchild asks, "Why?" — it is better to hesitate, and falter and stammer, than to grab easy answers and false explanations. Mythological thinking will

result, and the monistic mode of thinking and feeling may
be very helpful.

"It is all One."

"There is One."

"The All expresses itself in many ways."

"I am one of the ways, interconnected to all the other
ways, and so is everyone else."

"I do not understand what IT is doing."

"I remember, at least in this moment, the disparity
between the me and the not-me, in volume, in mass, in
age, in importance."

I will find myself speaking hesitantly to my grandchild,
especially in those situations when information isn't
exactly what is needed to answer that "Why?"
Unavoidably I find that I must speak mythologically.
Admitting that I'm not sure, that I don't know, will make
it easier all around in the long run. The monistic idea that
it is all one, all connected, may be of help.

B. Metaphor and Moratorium

Alcoholics Anonymous groups, and all the other anonymous organizations, including Gamblers, Narcotics, Smokers, Workaholics and Sexaholics, require that their participants turn their lives over to "a Higher Power." "You must acknowledge that you cannot control your own life, you need outside help, and you're ready to turn your life over to this Higher Power, for healing. In order to be free, you must admit that you can't handle alcohol, or gambling, or smoking, or work, or sex or whatever, and you must give your life into the hands of a Higher Power." At the same time the groups insist that they don't care how one defines, "Higher Power."

It works for many. These 12-step programs, as they are called, have better success rates than most other types of treatment for these various obsessions. But there are some people for whom the Higher Power is precisely the problem. "God" is the name of the obsession that they need liberation from. For a long time, while this book was in the early stages of writing and rewriting, I called it, "God Anonymous."

The carelessness about defining "Higher Power" may be causing some of the difficulty. We'll have to do our defining very carefully, and if what we've been calling "God" is really the Higher Power, we're still in trouble.

115

The obsession with God, poorly defined, can lead people to believe things that aren't true, and to do things that are unjust, and unkind. Popes, who punished Galileo and Copernicus and Teillard de Chardin for sharpening our awareness of truth, had this obsession. Both the perpetrators and some of the victims of the tortures of the Spanish Inquisition had this obsession. The perpetrators and some of the victims of the officially approved lynching of "witches" in Massachusetts suffered from it.

Modern persons who believe and act out their belief that God sent AIDS to punish homosexuals have it. Modern persons who believe that God is a male slave-holding dictator have it.

Persons who are afraid to do anything pleasant or fun, for fear that God would disapprove, have it. They seldom experience what we would call fun, but find their own type of entertainment in busily interfering with other people's attempts to find pleasure and satisfaction in life.

Persons who believe and act as though they really were special favorites of God, and then wonder why other people don't like them much, have this obsession.

And all these people will have difficulty escaping from this obsession by appealing to a Higher Power. Their understanding of the Higher Power is precisely the problem.

Recall the distraught young mother, joining in the God-is-dead controversy a couple of decades ago. She exclaimed, "Oh, I know there's a God — he's after me!" She believed that God was causing all the major and minor disasters that her life consisted of, that God was watching her, and picking on her, and thinking up and then carrying out plans to make her life miserable. She would have been better off without God. She would have been relieved to find a God Anonymous group, but there was no such thing, and anyway her concept of the Higher Power was precisely the problem.

The temptation is to decide that there is no Higher Power at all. The yearning is to be free of it, free at last. The inclination is to conclude that all God-material is baloney, or worse, and grow up and grow out of it, and learn to get along without it.

Many do this. They'll tell you, if you ask them, "You and I are lost in a huge meaningless cosmos. Don't bother searching for meaning, because there isn't any."

But there is a high price for this freedom. Justice becomes a mockery. Cosmic justice, that is. "Human justice" is already a contradiction in terms, by every indication. Law school students are taught, on the first day of classes, that the main question is, "How much justice can you afford?" Love without any cosmic meaning becomes sentimental and ridiculous, an unwise investment of energy, resources and time. Gratitude becomes superfluous. The sense of wonder atrophies. Ego, the doomed, ridiculous, paltry human ego, triumphs for its brief moment and then perishes forever and is forgotten.

This price is too high. The effort required to redefine "God" or "Higher Power" will have to be spent after all. So we may as well get at it.

"God" is a word. To what does that word refer? The rampant confusion about this can be seen on the way different people use the word. Pat Robertson, Albert

Schweitzer, Oliver North, Pope John XXIII, William
Penn, Ronald Reagan and William S. Coffin, all use the
word "God," but they aren't all referring to the same
thing. "Which God?" becomes a very fine question. We
can begin to grasp this when we see that "God" is not an
entity at all, but an idea. Not everyone who uses the word
is referring to the same idea, by any means.

"God" is a metaphor. Consider the most commonly-
used images for God: Judge, Potter [maker, creator],
Shepherd, King, Lord [owner, slave-master], Father.
These are all metaphors. Liberation begins when we
realize that all these metaphors make slaves, toys, sheep,
objects or victims out of most of us. The ones who gain
most from this God-idea are: kings, popes, owners,
dictators, authorities, parents. But it's a metaphor. We
may quit using it, if we want to.

Careful study of the Cosmos has not yet revealed a
Maker, set apart from what was made. The Maker has not
yet been located. The idea of a Creator and the Creation
comes from the fact that humans make things, like tools
and toys, but that may not be the best metaphor for
explaining Reality.

One could make a case for a different idea. Let's say
that "God" does not refer to an Entity, different from the
world, separate from the world, who made the world.
Let's let "God" refer to The Whole Thing, All of it, with
all its interconnectedness. Let's say "God" refers to What
There Is, As It Is, Doing What It Does. "God" could be
a code word for THAT.

Hindus do this. We have noted already that the
Christian theologian Paul Tillich tried it, calling "God,"

not a "Being," but "the Ground of All Being." "God" does not exist, because he is not a Being. He is the "Ground" of Being, of all existence. It was too far out for most Christians. Tillich was dismissed by most as a "pantheist." The idea of What There Is, As It Is, Doing What It Does is hard to sustain, and hard to talk about at any length. And it is hard to stick to that meaning, using the word, "God." "God" is too easy a word to substitute. It's too quick, too glib, too widely used in other ways. Some use it as an expletive and mean almost nothing at all when they say it. Most are dragging in some or all of that blatantly preposterous and erroneous formerly-accepted mythological content, all those stories of thrones, thunderbolts, jealousy, petulance, inscrutable meanness, revenge, meaningless testing. The pronoun "he" is a metaphorical anthropomorphism, which has caused great trouble for half of humanity. It would perhaps be easier to refer to THAT as "X," the unknown quantity. It would not contain such volumes of error as the word "God."

I propose a moratorium on the use of the word "God," say for a century or so. Let's force ourselves to stammer and define our terms and wave our arms in frustration. Let's force ourselves to hesitate, with "uh," and "um," and "OM." Let's drop that glib monosyllable, so easy to say, so useful for beating other folks over the head, so easy to ask forgiveness of and keep in our back pockets as a secret weapon, so easy to mock.

Let's drop it, and see what happens. Let's see if fresh clarity doesn't result, along with additional compassion for each other without interference from irrational authority. As long as we don't, we'll have to plow through heavy tomes on "the motherhood of God," "the will of God as revealed exclusively to the priesthood," "God and intelligent non-terrestrial life," "God and the theology of dolphins," "what God thinks about nuclear war, or smoking, or in vitro fertilization, or surrogate mothers, or sinful bishops," or dozens of other topics.

Letting go of this obsession will liberate the general human discussion which we need to have about all these things. And the liberation which individual humans can discover, when this obsession is dropped, will make us feel like new persons.

Most people who feel the need to overcome an oppressive God-obsession learned what they need to unlearn from some form of Christianity or Judaism. Oriental religions seem to be much less harmful, in this sense. They don't have the Creator/God, who turns into an autocratic unreasonable omnipotent authority figure.

The lore from the East describes how the Cosmos, over vast stretches of time, blinks on and off, alternating between stages of Being and Non-Being. We are in a Being phase, temporarily. Many observers have noted similarities between Oriental myth and modern scientific cosmology — the Big Bang can be thought of as the change from Non-Being to Being. Theories of a "final" implosion of all matter sound like the shift from Being to Non-Being. Oriental myth differs with modern science in insisting that nothing is final; the cycle of on/off continues infinitely.

In any case, when we go into the next Non-Being phase, What There Is could be called The Void. It won't be doing anything. But all potential Being, all possibilities, will be contained in that Void.

The God-question, for those who can't let go of the notion, can be put in this way: Does the Void, that which precedes all Being, and into which all temporary forms and all Being itself will return — does that Void also permeate Being, while we're in the Being phase? Is that Void present somehow here and now in such a way that paltry temporary forms, like you and me, can be aware of it? Can we get in touch with it, somehow?

Answer: Who knows? Maybe. Maybe not. Probably not, maybe. Certainty about this seems highly unlikely, except for some in certain moments of heightened awareness.

Persons into advanced meditation techniques come back with what they report feels like certainty. They have some kind of awareness of IT. They claim to have made some kind of contact with THAT. That Void.

It can safely be said that such contact or awareness is by no means universal. Not all temporary forms can be aware, or are aware, of any such direct experience of that Void.

Also, any temporary forms, like you and me, who are thus aware will be completely unable to prove anything at all to all those other temporary forms that are not yet aware of it.

Persons who make contact with, or stumble onto some awareness of, the Void are left speechless. Wise ones have urged that silence is always the correct response. "Those who know do not speak. Those who speak do not know."

Attempts to talk about it, to describe the Void, which are almost irresistible, are always unsatisfactory. What can

you say about it? The Void has no attributes at all. All
attempts to define that Void are in error. IT is not big, not
small, not fat, not thin, not green, not old, not polite, not
cruel, not anything! Attempts to name it fail. Attempts to
depict it fail.

But humans keep attempting, because we do want to
talk about whatever it is that the sense of wonder makes
us aware of. The wise advice is to be silent, but we
cannot.

The ancient Greek philosopher, Empedocles, who was
into geometry, gave a definition of the Absolute which
many find fascinating and even helpful. "'God' [even he
used that word which I think we need to discard] is a
circle whose center is everywhere and whose
circumference is nowhere." There's a real Uncertainty
Principle for you. This clears up any attempts to locate
IT, or confine IT, or make IT into someone's private
property.

Organized religions are based on supposed earlier
contacts with the Void, made by persons who died
afterward, but came to be highly revered later. The
organizations all fall short of whatever "meaning" that
original contact contained. Theology, synods, councils,
encyclicals, canons, sermons, legends about saints — none
of that is IT. Thomas Aquinas, near the end of his life,
had some kind of inner experience, and stopped writing.
He then referred to all his previous written tomes,
impressive attempts to organize all human knowledge,
including the "knowledge of God," as "so much straw."

Those of us needing relief from the God-obsession will
find many things cleared up, if we can imagine that Void,

and even seek heightened awareness of it, without calling it "God." That word simply is no longer helpful. There is too much erroneous baggage, derived from anthropomorphic myth we no longer believe, attached to the word "God." Laws, authority, jealousy, paternity — these things are not attributes of THAT. All those attempts to assign attributes come from the area of temporary forms, where we live and move and have our being, and they will all be swallowed up in the Void, at the next oscillation from Being to Non-Being.

C. S. Lewis once declared, "Everything is a subject on which there is not much to be said." I have to disagree with him. Lewis certainly had a very great deal to say about "God," but he did not equate "everything" and "God." He would have quickly dismissed that notion as pantheism. But the label alone is no excuse for leaving off thinking.

Since he had so little to say about "everything" — what I want to call What There Is, As It Is, Doing What It Does — and so very much to say about "God," I suspect that he is providing additional evidence that "God" is a lesser concept, a part and not the whole, and thus an idol.

Yet The Whole Thing does need talking about, and the fumbling, faltering circumlocutions are better and safer than monosyllables, like "God," or even "IT."

As we have noted, "God" carries with it all that erroneous content from all the myths, and is almost always really an idol. "It" leaves out the personal/gender factors which somehow need to be included, but either "He" or "She" is obviously one-sided and wrong. If we have to choose between "He" and "She," "She" would be more fair for a while, just because the emphasis has been grossly over-weighted the other way for millennia. Sometimes I use "IT" in a special tone of voice, as a short-cut code word for What There Is.

The objection to pantheism comes mostly from those who want to preserve the prerogatives of an institution which claims some kind of exclusive access to some supposedly saving power. Once the institution is dropped, pantheism looks rather inviting.

"God" has not abandoned India, China and Japan. "He" is known there as Buddha, Brahmin, Tao, No-Thing, The Void. All that vast tradition cannot be dismissed as sin and error, except by persons who have a vested interest in some sort of exclusive institution, some church.

My personal trouble with pantheism is in the logical inference that if everything is God, there is no need to dedicate one's life and efforts to anything, there is no worthy cause, there is no evil to combat. I have trouble with that, observing the world around me. Some things appear to be evil. The Nuclear Weapons stockpile, for instance, and the nuclear waste created in the manufacture of those weapons — aren't they evil? Their effect on humanity and on the Biosphere are evil. They need to be renounced and dealt with, and shame and regret will help get us motivated, maybe. If pantheism means that it's all God, and that it's all all right, all somehow the Will of God, then I'm put off. I don't think there's any God to it, really. There is human error and human crime. We'll get ahead sooner, if we proceed without the word "God," and without the *"theos"* in "pantheism."

I come back to the sense of wonder. Doesn't What There Is inspire wonder? Reality is awesome. The distances, the time, the marvelous interaction of everything — do we need an anthropomorphic "God" in there to lead us to sense wonder? I, frankly, think he's a hindrance.

"IT," all of it, is precisely what needs contemplating. Gnostics, ancient and modern, speak of The All. San Juan de la Cruz used the phrase *El Todo* [the All], meaning "What-there-is-the-way-it-is." "God" has been a code-word at best, too facile, too quickly shifted off target. Too easily and quickly it means something less than The All. Too soon it means a Being, a Part, a Particle, one-thing-over-against-other-things. IT doesn't mean that. IT means, "Everything. One Thing."

C. What Kind of Cosmos Is This?

The sense of wonder is activated when we become more deeply aware of the world we are part of. The cosmos is very large, if not infinite, and very old, if not eternal. Most of the myths of the world, except the Hebrew/Christian one, tell of cycles, roundness, repetition and recurrence. The Whole Thing goes round and round. The image of the Spiral, used in many traditions, suggests that the round-and-round repetition is not meaningless, but that a kind of upward or onward progress is at least possible.

The non-Christian traditions suggest that there is plenty of time in which we, and the Cosmos as a whole, can learn things. Life is not what some people say it is — a one-shot test, pass/fail, in which, if you flunk, you're damned, and most folks flunk. That notion came from the mean-hearted branch of Christianity. The Cosmos doesn't seem to operate on that basis. Repeated cycles, repeated opportunities, appear to be the norm.

The universe is full of intelligence, seething with it. The structure of the atom and the structure of nebulae indicate an underlying intelligent order. The more we study Chaos, the more we see repeated patterns in the midst of apparent randomness.

More and more thoughtful observers indicate that they

suspect that the Universe is full of life, as well as intelligence, that life did not evolve only on this one planet. There are two billion suns in our galaxy, and at least two billion other galaxies. The larger the known universe is found to be, the more likely it is that life has arisen in other places also.

For myself, it is helpful to state simply, "The Cosmos is intelligent, and it is alive." These attributes were not inserted into it by an outside entity. They simply describe what it is.

The Cosmos is motivated, set into motion, let's say, not only by mechanical forces like gravitation, but by something which can be called Desire. It can be seen at the atomic level, in the chemical bonds caused by the attraction and repulsion of electrons in the outer ring around each atomic nucleus. Positive and negative can even be personified as male and female. The sodium atom "wants" to get rid of that extra electron. The chlorine atom "wants" to take in one more electron to complete the outer ring. It almost looks like sexual attraction, and sexual behavior, between atoms!

And Desire is rampant, once life appears. Paramecia conjugate, exchanging nuclear materials. It looks sexual, when seen under a microscope. Gametes join, forming new organisms. The pressure on the individual organisms of the "higher" forms to arrange for and allow for this joining of gametes verges on the irresistible. "Find a way to reproduce before you die," seems to be the law of life forms. Theological attempts to hinder this pressure, which builds up in humans as well as all other life forms, have resulted mostly in failure and tragedy. Theologians have

been trying for ages to disapprove of the kind of Cosmos
we find ourselves a part of, without much success.

There are two special areas that need additional
consideration in connection with this question about the
kind of Cosmos we are in.

Justice

Is the Cosmos just? Is there any justice, anything like
Cosmic Justice? One of the metaphors for "God" is that of
Judge. He claims the task of putting some kind of
evaluation on human life. The Hebrew prophets related
this function of Judge to large human groups, like nations,
and declared that at the root of the judgment meted out by
history was some sense of fairness, some sense of Higher
Justice. For us, the question is, "Were the prophets on to
something more than their own wishful thinking?"

Later the concept of judgment was applied to individual
human lives, and then moved to some point after the end
of the terrestrial life span, and we ended up with the
Cosmic Bookkeeper, and large numbers of people who
were afraid to do anything at all for fear of spoiling their
chances at some posthumous reward. The point the
prophets were trying to make was being missed, by all.

Socrates said, "The unexamined life is not worth
living." He's saying that each one of us has the obligation
to examine his or her own life. He does not push that
function off onto some external Entity, who will judge
from the outside after the end. The Christian tradition puts
the emphasis on posthumous judgment, and over the
centuries has used it to browbeat and frighten people into

obedience. Fear of cosmic punishment has kept the poor and the oppressed in a state of quiescence for centuries. Karl Marx saw all this more than a century ago, and dealt with it by assuming that the Cosmic Judge wasn't there at all, and encouraged workers to chuck the whole idea. "You have nothing to lose but your chains."

The Cosmic Bookkeeper became little more than a joke. He is the *Dim-Witted God* described earlier — foolish, easy to fool, easy to bribe. But must the sense of Cosmic Justice be tossed out with the metaphor of the Cosmic Bookkeeper? Does the Cosmos "keep track"? In the Orient, the concept of karma deals with this question that we are asking. What one does has a long-term ripple effect, creates long-term consequences, and comes back to help determine things later. It is mostly automatic, not applied by a personal judge. Instead, it is built into the structure of things.

We have this same idea, in our science. We call it cause-and-effect. "Every action causes an equal and opposite reaction." Newton said that, and physicists demonstrate it with billiard balls. Students of the pendulum have noted it, also. "The swing to the left equals the swing to the right." It's physics, not morality. There is no should to it. It simply is. The Cosmos is totally interconnected to itself. Everything that happens ramifies outward in all directions. Pluck a flower and you influence a star.

Thinking like this led to what was called "determinism," the idea that whatever is happening now was determined entirely by what happened before, that it is all irrevocably unavoidable, and not subject to free-will influence. That is, even if you are inclined to interfere and influence the course of events, that's so only because you, too, have been predetermined by events in your past.

Very few persons have really accepted this notion that everything is inevitable and there's no use trying to better things. Determinism drops God out of the picture, and also all our earnest effort. Some Christians were able to keep both God and determinism in place, by stating that God had personally predetermined everything. Some thought it worthwhile to distinguish between the deity's foreknowledge of everything and his predetermination of events. That was because they didn't want to blame things like Adolph Hitler on God. They didn't want to say that all that evil was his doing, even though the Bible in several places says it is, in effect. Everything that happens is something God is doing, it says.

"God hardened the heart of Pharaoh." Pharaoh didn't do all those bad things himself, it says. He was, by inference, hardly responsible for his own actions, in not letting the Israelites go until after all the plagues had been visited upon Egypt. He was putty in the hands of God.

But what shall we think and do, we who have let the idea of "God" go? Is there some kind of natural automatic arrangement which we could call Justice? The old alchemists, who believed in it, called it The Undeviating Justice. They believed it was in place, and working. I must say I'm drawn to the idea.

If it isn't automatic and impersonal, it would be subject to abuse. There would be Cosmic Lawyers, ranting about extenuating circumstances, reasonable doubt, loopholes, prerogatives, executive privilege, exceptions to the rule and statutes of limitations. But the Cosmos runs by cause and effect, not by these legalistic fine points. What goes up must come down. What goes around comes around. Garbage in, garbage out. If we could improve on the current "automatic" arrangement, one could wish for two things:

[1] "Too bad ignorance isn't painful."

[2] "Too bad it sometimes takes so long for causes to have their effects."

The first is obvious. If ignorance were painful, people would change destructive behavior quicker. The second is where The Undeviating Justice loses many thoughtful people. My friend Dan, the Potter, said, "I question whether it's true locally." I replied that it was strange to me that he would put it spatially. For me, I suspect that The Whole Thing may be just indeed, but over time spans that make the average human lifetime insignificant. In other words, it is the human ego that may not get just treatment, and egos can't imagine what else would matter. "Oh, that's exactly what I mean by 'locally,'" Dan said.

The God-obsessed have victimized themselves and others by prating about "sin," as if one person could thoroughly understand and make rules for another. General rules have been set up, about causing deliberate harm to oneself and others, and immediately the casuists go to work on the exceptions and the extenuating circumstances. I think much good would result, if we dropped the word "sin," since we as a species insist on changing the meaning of the word. It originally meant "missing the mark," "aiming, shooting and missing." But it has come to mean "bad deed," subject to endless cataloging, mortal, venal, deadly and all that, to be atoned for by dying on the cross, or by saying ritual prayers, or by self-inflicted punishment in the form of self-hate.

On the other hand belief in the Undeviating Justice is somewhat scary. There are no exceptions, no explanations, no excuses. Causes have their effects, simply. In comparison to The Undeviating Justice, Zeus and YHWH can be swayed, which makes it all unjust.

Americans had better be praying that God is not just, or that there is no such thing as a just God. If there is, then overt and covert actions in Iran, Guatemala, the Congo, Vietnam, Cambodia, Laos, Mozambique, Angola, Nicaragua, Cuba, El Salvador, Chile, Argentina, Panama and Iraq mean there is trouble up ahead for Americans. Many of the perpetrators of all that wickedness, persons like Oliver North, take refuge in their belief in a tin-horn God who is nothing like The Undeviating Justice.

Truth

Another basic question comes to mind. Is this a Cosmos in which Truth matters? Perhaps that is a question only a human could ask.

Trees don't lie. Rocks don't lie. Bees don't lie. Whales don't lie. I recall being stunned when I found an anthropologist's hypothesis, that the function of human language was to lie. The evolutionary advantage of the development of human language was deception, he suggested. The hypothesis never caught on, never went very far in the profession, although the same idea was behind the brief interest in "body language." The tongue can lie, but the rest of the body cannot, or, more precisely, unless you pay attention and take control, your body's position and movements will betray your true intentions even as your mouth lies.

Dolphins have language — do they lie? Has the navy taught them that human trick?

The Cosmos, as a whole, seems lined up on the side of Truth. Nature, however, includes some remarkable things, like protective coloration, which is deception. Nobody here but us soot-colored moths in this sooty world. This is just sunlight and shadows in the leaves, not a leopard lying in wait for unaware passers-by.

Still, nature doesn't lie. Predators eat their prey. Plants outdo each other reaching for light. And human science, which tries to comprehend all that, when it hasn't been purchased by governments or corporations, doesn't lie. It seeks out Truth. It seeks to know How It Is.

The government agency can raise the "allowable" level of radiation, as the actual level of radiation is raised by the activities of that agency, but that doesn't change the effect that accumulated radiation actually has on living cell tissue. Radiation doesn't lie, and cells don't lie. Paid spokespersons for agencies and paid "scientists" hired by agencies do the lying.

"There is nothing secret that shall not be made known." Exposés of human radiation experiments, of celebrity shenanigans fifty years ago, of secret treaties and black budgets and covert operations — it is all bound to come to light eventually.

In personal, inner matters, I believe it is better to know than not know. I want to know the name of the disease —

if I ever suspect the family of lying to me "to protect me," I'll be furious. The inner exploration, the memories, the repressed pain and anger — I have learned that knowing is vastly better than not knowing. Ignorance is a faulty, stupid, childish kind of bliss.

The Cosmos is on the side of truth, even if individual human egos seem to thrive temporarily by lying, and even on being lied to. What is truth? Pontius Pilate asked that question at the pseudo-trial of Jesus of Nazareth. He pretended he didn't know, but he did. The truth was that this man was innocent, and Pilate was being pressured to pronounce him guilty. So Pilate pretends that the truth can't be known. Who did he deceive?

Here's a koan for persons brought up in the culture of Western Civilization, whether they're Christian or not: "How can one believe something is true, and *not* act accordingly?"

It was Dostoyevsky, replying to Nietzsche's assertion that God was dead, who wrote in **The Brothers Karamazov**: "without God, everything is permitted." He suggests that without God, there is no ethics, no morality. Everything is permitted. But that is not necessarily so. Humans could build an ethic, a system of morality, based simply on Truth.

The God of the fundamentalists is a weak straw on which to build ethics. Their leaders are far from paragons of ethical behavior. Note Jim Baaker, Jimmy Swaggart, Jerry Falwell, Oliver North. They are narrow-minded, mean-hearted, cruel, ruthless, quick to punish and quick to speak falsehood, bent on deception, and concerned more about image than truth. The world will be better off when all that is completely discredited, and we can get back to Truth, pure and simple.

Note how falsehood has corroded the legal system. Liars get away with murder. The bigger the lie, the more crime is allowed. Yet the Cosmos itself extracts a penalty. The stench of the very system itself will finally cause change, perhaps drastic change. If I ran the legal/penal system, it would be based entirely on recompense and restitution. No consideration of intent, or motives, no forgiveness, no bargaining, no pardon, no loopholes, no statutes of limitations — you did this, which harmed this person, so you owe this. "The piper must be paid." "You will never get out until you have paid the last penny." But don't worry, they won't set up my system. Note, however, that a system based on simple truth is imaginable. And Life, itself, is like that. Effects have causes. Causes produce effects.

William Blake observed something which must be considered. "Truth can never be told, so as to be understood, and not be believed." The sentence is nothing short of astonishing. I think of my own experiences, long ago. I used to preach what I sincerely believed was truth. People didn't believe what I told them. That means, either:

[1] I didn't tell it right, or
[2] They didn't hear it right, or
[3] It wasn't true!

What is truth? Pilate was pretending to justify his own evil actions when he asked that. But we need to ask it, whether we're under such pressure or not. Can Truth be known? And if so, what is it?

We're not in some self-service supermarket, selecting truth to suit our taste, our preference, our prejudices. There is not an array of truths, from which we may select one, or several. Truth, as Blake meant it, and as I'm trying to ascertain it, is not a purely personal matter.

I became alarmed in the midst of a conversation with a young student, who was majoring in "communication." I wondered aloud, "Is lying communication?" We debated as to how in the world a congenital liar could be The Great Communicator. We wondered if unintended messages also constitute communication. I wasn't sure the two of us were communicating. I seemed to be clinging to a thing called Truth, and she seemed to be thinking that everything was relative. If something other than information is passed across, is that communication? Is disinformation information? When she used the phrase, "false truth," I gave up. The mutually contradictory words meant that, for her, each person has his own private truth in his head or in his heart, and it could at the same time be pure Error, a false truth. For her, there is no final Truth, no absolute Truth.

But one must also ask, do we ever really have all the data in, so that Truth can be ascertained, and believed? Maybe Blake is falling into the same trap that grips the doctrinaire fundamentalists. He sounds so very sure. Is he suggesting that he knows, and we don't? Is there only one Truth?

The poem about the blind men and the elephant illustrates how partial truths can cause problems. C. S. Lewis states the problem his way in **The Silver Chair,** one of **The Chronicles of Narnia.** Jill wants and needs a drink badly, but is afraid of the huge lion lying between her and the delicious stream running by. "I'll just have to find another stream," she says.

The lion says, "There is no other stream." It's another version of "No man cometh unto the Father but by me." But Lewis is wrong about that. There are many streams. His own stream is his partial truth. There are many partial truths.

A study of world mythology will help one see that there is one underlying story, which all the myths are telling, imperfectly. And the clear lesson seems to be this. Continue the Search. Stay on the Path. Pay attention as you go. Search for more Truth. Do not become arrogant about how much you have found already. Truth exists. The cosmos runs by it. But you do not know it all yet.

The Myth That Failed

As we break free of the God-obsession, we are able to step back and take a better look at its source. It is the keystone of an elaborate myth which has held western civilization in its psychological grip since the days of the Emperor Constantine. Now we may evaluate that myth as a whole, and as we do so, we will see that it has failed in many different ways.

The Christian myth has failed to protect other races and cultures. Over the centuries it has actively sought to destroy those cultures and enslave those people. Northern Europe first, and then Africa and the Americas offer the evidence. The myth allowed, and in some instances encouraged, the conquests and enslavement.

The myth has failed to protect other species. The defenders of the buffalo, and the whales, and in our time the salmon, are not the Christians, but the people who are being overwhelmed by the Christians.

The myth has failed to protect the environment. It hardly considers the subject, as such. The environment is thought of as the scene in which God tests mankind, not as a living miraculous web of interconnections. It was people untroubled by the Christian myth who came up with that understanding. And in our day the new comprehension of our place in the web of life is essential. The old myth of man's dominion over nature, man's task and right to "conquer" nature, must be repudiated and abandoned, or the web of life will be destroyed.

The myth failed to express oneness, solidarity, open-mindedness, open-heartedness, harmony, fairness — these things do not characterize the history of this myth and of those who adhere to it. The secular humanists have shown what must be done and the hateful ragings of the fundamentalists against them simply underscore the obvious. The values of the secular humanists are what the world craves and needs, not the false slogans of cruel people.

The myth has failed to support individuals in need. It has failed to relieve individuals in pain. It has failed to defend individuals in trouble. Slaves, workers, women, children — all have been left out. Individual Christians have given their very lives to oppose war, care for lepers, and feed the hungry, but the myth itself, and the powerful institutions it has brought into being have had little effect, and invested precious little interest in anything beyond perpetuating themselves.

As far as children are concerned, teaching them Christianity constitutes abuse, even if there is no overt sexual or physical abuse. An eating disorder counsellor finds many multiple personality cases, and an alarming percentage of them have roots in a childhood plagued with "abuse-and-religion." The counsellor uses the phrase as a single word, in the style of the anthropology professor who speaks of "magic-and-religion." She calls abuse and religion all one thing. Another sensitive friend refers to her childhood in which she was subjected to Christian indoctrination as simply "spiritual abuse."

To teach a child that he is a sinner, that the problems of the world are his fault, that he is not all right, that something is the matter with him, that this particular institution has the cure if he will obey and pay, and that if he's not cured it's his fault — all that constitutes abuse.

I have met parents who do not themselves believe in Christianity, yet they deliberately send their children to Christian Sunday School, thinking that it can do no harm and may do some good. They are wrong. It can and does do harm. It sets up a series of problems what will sooner or later have to be gotten over — self-hate, distrust of bodily instinct, misplaced allegiance, and the one we're dealing with here, the God-obsession. Children will be better off, if they are spared all that.

The Christian myth can also be faulted, I believe, for the way the God of that myth has been re-shaped to fit the times. Persons who know little of philosophy or theology, and who stay away from churches as a general rule, can be caught referring to "The Man Upstairs" with an upward roll of the eyeballs. It's a metaphor, and not a very good one, even though it is popular in contemporary stories. "The Man Upstairs" is usually described as very wise, perhaps all-knowing. He keeps track; he is the Cosmic Bookkeeper we have mentioned before. He somehow tends to things. It is not a good metaphor, however, because there is no upstairs to it, and whatever is being referred to, it is not a man.

The Man Upstairs is God, without any traditional theological content. Usually what is meant is that God is smarter, has a better perspective and more control of things than we downstairs ordinary mortals. There is seldom much ethical content to this Man Upstairs — I wonder what he thinks of nuclear stockpiling, cruelty, hypocrisy, or leaders who lie. When the old prophets talked about "The Lord God," you knew what *that* God thought about such subjects.

Why would people be tempted to want to use this inadequate metaphor? And where are the modern prophetic spokespersons of "The Lord God," who could keep the record straight? I suspect that this watering down has happened because people want a God they can handle, and maybe even deceive.

Our current obsession with secrecy is an indication of this. If there is an all-seeing, all-wise Deity watching and comprehending all things, why so much effort at deception? Presidents and military cabinet persons are upset about "leaks" and "publicity." They are terrified of the media. They work hard to prevent the discovery and dissemination of truth and they have formed Departments of Disinformation. The press must be controlled, they say.

Future wars will not be fought on television, they say. As if by hiding it, war could be made into something that good people would approve of.

At the same time these public officials talk a great deal about God. What kind of God do these hiders and deceivers have? Is he blind, after all? Is he not just, after all? Is he not Truth, after all?

The same thing surfaces closer to home. I know a lady who believes in God, yet she still tries to hide the fact that her husband steals, that her daughter is on dope, and that she herself has cancer. Who is she hiding all this truth from? Me? Herself, more likely. What about "God"? What about The Man Upstairs?

The Man Upstairs is an amazingly unsatisfactory metaphor. The name "God" isn't enough, not big enough, not inclusive enough. God is too tangled up with preposterous notions, relics of old myths, like robes and beards and thunderbolts and thrones and naked flying cherubs. But the name "God" ought not to mean that old man up there who may or may not understand. God should mean Reality. What There Is, As IT Is. IT is consistent with itself, and entirely in touch with itself. So that means that IT does understand, more dependably than God or any humanly contrived metaphor.

I suspect that it would be best for humans to search for more clarity on this before the last minute. Delivering one's "soul" to "God" at the end of life — what does that really mean, with neither term defined or even thought about? There's too much at stake to take the priest's or the pastor's word for it. And how does *he* know? Isn't this something that each one should do for himself or herself?

"Delivering one's soul to God" can be a very fine metaphor. It can mean that the dying person believes that the Cosmos is a safe place, that I accept my mortal limitations, that I have given living a good try, that it was "worth it." It can even mean that I believe that whatever is on the other side, if anything, will be good for me, just as life has been. But I need more than The Man Upstairs to assure me of that. I need galaxies and evolution and black holes and electrons and osmosis and heat and light and consciousness and will and love.

Consider again The Undeviating Justice. Heavier-than-air machines fly, not because they are excused from the law of gravity, but because of an improved understanding of that very law. If you know How-It-Is, you can do wonders. But The Undeviating Justice is a far cry from The Man Upstairs. Nevertheless it can be believed, believed in, understood — more and more fully. The problem is it requires a longer view, a very much longer view than one small human ego-centered lifetime. In the East they call it Karma — you get what's coming to you. And whatever you get, you had it coming to you. If you do believe this, it'll make you put your life in order. Believing in God *should* do that, but notice how often it doesn't.

A North American church group was studying Central America and the cause of all the unhappiness there. One member expressed himself with striking honesty. "I used to believe in equality. But now that I've learned how much my life-style depends on the uneven distribution of the world's goods, I don't believe in it anymore." One must assume, also, that he doesn't believe in God, much less The Undeviating Justice, which will even things out sooner or later.

It may be easier for members of blatantly oppressed groups to believe in The Undeviating Justice. For straight white male imperialist Americans I suspect it may have an unpleasant ring to it. I know it does for me.

D. What Kind of Person Do I Want To Be?

As we break free of the God-obsession, we discover a new opportunity, which is also a new responsibility. Instead of being a pawn in the hands of Someone Else, we find ourselves in charge of our own lives. The new sensation can be daunting at first. "You mean I have to decide? You mean it's simply up to me?"

The most basic question of all becomes, "What kind of person do I want to be?" It may sound strange, for a while, to think that I have this person to take care of, this person which is myself.

Dependence and Maturity

The God-obsession keeps a person dependent, or in a dependent state of mind. Old child-parent relationship patterns are preserved, by projecting the Parent onto the Cosmos. Our Heavenly Father tends to things, but he expects us to report in more or less all the time. Prayers are meant to be acts of submission. Sometimes they turn into attempts to give information to the supposed Source of all Wisdom and Knowledge in the Universe. When you think about it, that's comical. Attempts to hide things from that same Source are just as funny.

But the attitude, the state of mind, is what concerns us

here. The very language of the obsession keeps one weak and stupid and little and irresponsible. As a mere boy Jesus said, "I must be about my father's business," and we're expected to imitate him. Now that I'm an adult, what about my own business? We used to say, "I belong to Mother Church." But now I find I am weaned and on my own.

Churches and groups have a way of enforcing this dependence. If you show signs of growing up and thinking things through for yourself and making up your own mind and daring to run your own life, you may have to distance yourself from church or group, at least for a while, because they'll be trying to make you feel that you are a traitor, lonely and scared.

What you were supposed to believe was already determined, by the dogmas and the confessions and the councils and the creeds. You didn't need to think for yourself, or decide what your own premises are going to be for your own thinking and deciding. Adherents are expected to let God and church do that for them.

What is to be done has also been decided and fixed already. The commandments, the rules, the canon laws have already been written. A recent survey showed that 80% of American teenagers polled believe that The Ten Commandments are valid rules for living — and that 3% of those persons could name them! There's dependency for you. Depend on a set of rules, without even knowing what they are. Of course, people don't do what the rules say, anyway. For example, the commandment about killing precludes our paying our taxes to the Pentagon, but most of us pay them anyway. The commandment against stealing forbids unequal taxes and excess profits, and if the nation obeyed, the economy would collapse. The commandment against false witness would shut down advertising, publicity, news conferences, talk-show ranting and all forms of indoctrination. The prohibition of graven images would shut down art itself. Covetousness, like stealing, keeps the economy going and growing.

The rules are fixed, for those who like rules. Most people give only lip-service to the church's rules. So the rules are broken. Then the God-obsession and the churches excuse people and forgive them, so that everything can continue in the same old way, with the people in a state of dependence.

Thinking for oneself and being responsible for one's decisions are not encouraged by the God-obsession and its institutions. An outward appearance of obedience to legalistic rules without rocking the boat is much preferred. Growth and pioneering and questioning and experimenting and daring and risking all make trouble.

The God-obsession instead offers security. "I Need Jesus." "I Need Thee Every Hour." One is even encouraged to think of oneself as a sheep. "The Lord Is My Shepherd." Not merely a sheep, but lost sheep. "All we like sheep have gone astray." It is not at all flattering, but once it's spotted, it can be outgrown.

The great boon that Jesus supposedly offers — escape from hell — is a kind of fire insurance. Maybe you're not sure that the loving God really would put you or anyone into the hellfire of eternal conscious torment, but just in case, just to be sure, better take out a modest, not-too-expensive policy. It becomes a combination of dependency, dishonesty and laziness.

Dependence, fear, infantilism, childishness, believing nonsensical fairy tales, yearning for Mamma, trying still to obey Daddy — it's all typical of the God-obsession. And now we must watch out for another trick. When exceptions to what I'm saying turn up — Teresa of Avila, Soren Kierkegaard, Martin Luther King, for example — God's people hate them while they're alive and then make saints of them after they're dead, and continue to refuse to take them seriously as persons who could challenge us to live free, daring, fruitful, just and loving lives.

The process of maturing is painful. It is seldom told how lonely it is. Some forego the experience and return to easy canned answers and instructions rather than go it alone. Some get out and become bitter hateful loners, and that's another tragedy. I was in danger of that for a while, after I tore myself out of the womb of mother-church and repudiated the authority of Nobodaddy. "Nobodaddy" is the name William Blake invented for the Projected Father Figure who isn't there, and I'm forever grateful for Blake's insight. I'll have to run my own life, I realized. I am the master of my fate. I am the captain of my soul.

No one followed me out of the womb of Holy Mother Church into the cold cruel world with intent to woo me back or pull me back in. I wanted out, so they let me out. They let me go. And I managed to be angry about that, too, even though it was exactly what I wanted. Nobody cares, I thought. They don't really give a damn about me. But they were doing exactly what I said I wanted them to do — leave me alone!

I was saved by sensuality and love. I accepted a new

dependence — on the Whole Thing, on Earth Herself, on soil and water and the other elements in the bio-sphere, and on a few loving people. It was a miracle. I was dead, and am alive again. I came to know what "newness of life" really means.

Treasure those who will love you without wanting to control you. They are precious. They may be few, but they can be found. If you think you're lacking loving persons around you, the old pop song can advise you:
"You're nobody, until somebody loves you...
So find yourself somebody — to love!"
Go after it actively, and be profoundly grateful for the love that comes your way. Respond to it. Don't push it away. But be a mature self-directed active lover, not a coddled, spoiled, need-directed, dependent recipient only.

Self-Hate and the Self

Perhaps the greatest disability caused by the God-obsession is self-hate. The process is begun early on by the God-people. The child learns that his body is bad and his thoughts are evil. Nowadays the process is carried forward by huge business corporations and their advertising messages.

The products of the body's elimination processes are evil, and smell bad, we are taught. Even sweat is evil, and smells bad, and the fact that it is a liquid must be hidden. And sex — I don't need to belabor the role of the perpetrators of the God-obsession in spoiling sex. Much of the freedom, so-called, of our time, in all the story-telling media, is still obsessive because it is an over-reaction. Many of the stories wallow in sex, and then end up with the same message — it is bad, not to be trusted, dirty, sordid and gross.

A healthy child, with a fully functioning body, runs the risk of becoming convinced that there's something wrong with him, because he must urinate and defecate, and he's curious about copulation — and he'd better not use the Anglo-Saxon words for any of that either! In my own childhood training, the words were more deadly and carried more tabu-force than the actual bodily facts of life. I could have a bowel movement, and even pass gas except in company, but the words "shit" and "fart" brought threats of a spanking.

The body is bad, but the thoughts are worse, according to the teaching. Desire, covetousness, sensuality, anger, self-assertion — all were very bad. Jealousy was a sin, and yet the double message was remarkable — compete and give it all you've got, try to be first, try hard to WIN, but don't feel anything, if you don't win, or even if you do. Jealousy of the winner is a sin. Or pride in being the winner is a sin. Win or lose, there was no way you could avoid sin.

That precisely was the intent of all that teaching, really — to make you feel like a sinner. You are guilty. Whatever you've done, you have sinned. In your very being you are a sinner. A sensitive person converts all this into self-hate.

Such an attitude is demoralizing, debilitating, and distracts the victims from the excitement of growing and learning. It's a blight on childhood that can spoil a whole lifetime. "I'm gonna hang myself, because I'm no damn good." During adolescence it can be extremely dangerous.

Some are so fearful of doing bad, they choose to do little or nothing. The Pharisees of Jesus' time handled life that way. Concentrate on not sinning. The best way is to do little, give no offense, stay out of trouble, live little and only tentatively, tip-toe through life feeling little and attempting little. Worry about how you're doing, even when you're not really doing anything of note at all. Freeze up Desire and turn off. It is a tragic waste of life, caused by self-hate.

There's a St.Peter-at-the-gate story which tries to combat this. A fellow arrived, wanting admission. Peter asked him what he had done. His reply listed all he had not done — never did this, never did that. Almost all the commandments tell you what not to do, and he hadn't done any of them. "Never made me any graven images." Peter was furious. "You never did anything! You never lived at all! Go back, and do something!"

The prayers of confession refer not only to sins of commission, things you did, but also sins of omission, things you didn't do that you should have. So there's no way out. A sensitive person gets it from all sides, no matter what he does.

Whatever combination of good sense, logic, love, weariness, self-assertion and circumstance brings it about, the process of outgrowing self-hate may well look like selfishness, and we've been taught that that's a bad thing. "Always thinking of yourself first." "You've become very self-centered."

The words are tricky in this area. If selfishness means walking all over other people in total disregard for their worth or their feelings or their needs, then it is not a good thing. But if someone has begun to doubt that he or she is all bad, and shows signs of taking charge of his or her life, to do something with it, to change it for the better, we need to look carefully. The people who are screaming, "Selfishness!" may be those who stand to lose a patsy, an unpaid servant, a footmat, an object taken quite for granted up to now. The worm is turning!

The Self requires some attention. Self-defense, self-preservation and especially self-love — there's a place for all that. If you don't love your Self, you'll not get anywhere trying to love anyone else. You'll be a whimpering, whining, manipulator of the people around you, maybe, but that's not love.

Love yourself. Affirm your essential goodness, and beauty. Your sweat, your urine, your fecal matter, your menstrual blood, your semen — affirm them all. They are good! You don't need to throw them at people, but you are permitted to stop being ashamed of them.

And listen to an old verse. "What doth it profit a man, if he gain the whole world and lose his own self?" The old translation was "soul," but it means self. Exactly that. Your Self. Your essence. What you are. What makes you tick. Your very being. For starters, stop hating it. And next, stop selling it and risking it and wasting it in activities and relationships that do not affirm it and support it.

"Ego" is a superficial, pretentious fiction we carry around — mostly it's what we think of ourselves when other people are nearby and looking. What will the neighbors think? What will the family think? "Self" is what you are, when you're alone, and thinking heavy thoughts and experiencing the archetypal crises of life. Ego is fickle, changing all the time, adapting to fashion and to what other people think or say. Ego cares a great deal about the temporary advantages and losses that come and go. Ego wants to live forever, and won't. Ego is what the God-obsession appeals to. "Eternal life." "Salvation." If those concepts mean that this ego persists on and on, then they are leading people astray.

But the Self — that's another matter. The Self is an expression of The All. The-Whole-Thing has a Self, and you are It. So am I. So is she. That humble bow with the hands clasped together, upon meeting a stranger in India, expresses the wonder of that. Each of us is that. You are that. Our loyalty can be to THAT, not to ego. We can live for that, and nothing less than that. The Whole Thing. Our devotion is for All-of-It — not some part, not even that proud comical little ego we carry around, and certainly not somebody else's.

Pride, and Judging

In the Hebrew/Christian tradition the original sin was pride. The root of sin is pride. What's the meaning of those old teachings? Now that we've gotten rid of the Cosmic Bookkeeper and his threats of punishment, won't that unleash more pride than ever? Won't getting rid of this infantile obsession make me more dangerously proud than ever?

The Greeks worried about pride as much as the Jews. They called it "hubris." Their myths and dramas teach how deadly it is. Arrogance will destroy the one who displays it. Haughty airs of superiority, reckless use of power and position, reaching too high and too far, believing that you're better than others in essence and not merely in circumstance — it'll do you in, and many other people will be badly hurt before the story's ended. Even the gods had to beware of "hubris."

I don't believe either the Jews or the Greeks were wrong in their assessment of pride. It is still deadly. Much of my quarrel with the God-obsession as I've observed it in myself and others is precisely that it feeds pride. It has had the exact opposite effect from what it pretends to try to do. This has worked on a personal as well as a cultural level.

The God-obsession teaches that God cares about me. I am saved. I am chosen. I am elect. Much of my own personal response to all that teaching was an exaggerated sense of duty and mission. If God cares so much about me, it's because he wants me to do this, and this, so let's get at it and do it and let's keep at it. I'm convinced now that the exaggerated seriousness and zeal and the faulty sense of humor that characterized my behavior then were caused by pride. I was a better servant of the Lord than these others. I was really more obedient. I worked harder at it. I was a really good investment of God's saving grace, I thought deep inside myself.

There can be little doubt that the God-obsession contributes greatly to our cultural pride. We're better than other people, and have the right to lord it over them and live better than they do and get paid better than they do for less strenuous effort, because we have God on our

side. We are God's people. We are his chosen, his
favorites. This is obviously idolatry, but it is also pride.
It is arrogance. And it is gross error. It would be
downright comical, if it could be viewed from a neutral
angle, but it is infuriating, if you're one of the victims of
that kind of attitude and the behavior it leads to. And
therefore it is dangerous, causing hostile feelings and
violent reactions.

I do not believe getting rid of the God-obsession will
increase pride. It may reduce it, by putting each one down
naked in the midst of the Cosmos with no mythological
protector. It will take away arrogance, and give dignity.
I am not better, but I am me, and I am of worth, and I
don't need to take abuse from anybody. To get rid of fear,
to get past the weakness and littleness of childhood, to get
rid of an obsession that hinders living, to see the myth
behind the veil — that won't make you better than other
people. But it will free you to regard them fairly and
objectively and lovingly and maturely.

Judging others is caused by being uncertain of
ourselves. Judgmental persons need someone to look down
on. Busybodiness, backbiting and gossip are fun for
persons whose own lives are purposeless and painfully
dull. They cannot put themselves into other people's
moccasins enough to care about the pain such behavior
causes.

So many of the "helping" projects which people do in
the name of God have pride at the root. The help isn't
really there until the victim cringes and grovels. The help
all too often consists of telling the other guy what he's
done wrong, telling him how to live, telling him what to

change and what to do. So much of the help is words, words, words. Advice. Sermons. Counsel. One who knows is telling the other dumb jerk How-It-Is.

I became less prone to "help," when I left all that. I was told plainly enough, in more than one instance, that the black liberation movement, in which I had been involved, didn't need my help. Instead, I needed to help my fellow white folks get off other people's backs and let them be truly free to help themselves. And besides, I needed to help myself, and I don't mean by grabbing things. I needed to help myself grow up, muster the courage to confront the world without God, get my own life put together, and make sure I wasn't in other people's way. I needed to quit judging other people.

God-obsessed people tend to be judgmental. They know what God wants, especially for other people. They have a keen sense of "justice," which they wield in a prejudiced way in the name of God. But what about Justice itself? With no such God in the picture, for the likes of us, where will Justice come from? Is there any such thing?

I find myself unable to prove it — it's like the existence of God used to be. I have to gamble on something not proven, but I find myself wanting to believe and trying to believe that the Cosmos Itself is Just.

I see it in physics. What goes up must come down. The swing to the right equals the swing to the left. Every action has an equal and opposite reaction. It feels uncomfortably mechanical, at times, but at least it's fair, and virtual particles allow that it may not be all quite so rigidly fixed as first appears. It is certainly more fair than anything that human judges can manage, or Nobodaddy, or judgmental believers in Nobodaddy.

Effects have causes. I have spent great hunks of time and energy, tracing backward in my own life, looking for the causes of this effect, this effect which is my life. I have uncovered some very interesting material, but I have also learned that old past causes verge on the irrelevant. They can't be nailed down precisely, and if they could, what would I do with them? I still have to come back to right here and now and the illusion, if it is an illusion, that I have choices to make and decisions to decide.

Causes have effects. What I do now ramifies in all directions forever. When I was a teacher, the students used to ask me, "Does this count, Sir?" They referred to some exercise, some quiz, in a harshly grade-oriented school. This teacher used to tease them good-naturedly, growling, "Every breath you take counts, Kid. So pay attention."

Everything we do has its effect. An unkind word, a cup of cold water, a smile, a chop — they cause results, whether anyone is keeping track, or not. Results occur, whether credit or recompense ever gets all the way back to the source, or not. Given all the time and all the distance and all the possibilities and all the order and all the "information," and all the things I do not comprehend at all — I can still believe it is all Just. I find I'm still living "by faith," after all, or trying to.

I'll admit sometimes I have trouble hanging on to it. I see innocent people mangled in the ego-games of generals and politicians. I see the "common man" vote as if the only value left was his own personal monetary gain, and I'm convinced he's in error even about that! I see crooks and liars getting away with it, and I do not believe that there's a Daddy-O in the sky who is going to stop them. I think maybe you and I will have to stop them, but I admit I sometimes don't know quite how to proceed.

So I come back to my own little life. I try to let it be a tiny little agent for Justice. And Kindness. I don't always succeed. This sounds uncomfortably like things the Apostle Paul and I said in the old days — I know what to do, but I don't always do it!

I must submit to The Cosmos, finally. The Whole Thing is all right. They can't really injure it, nor can I. It is expressing Itself in all these ways, even in those crooks and liars who seem to be driving things to ruin. And It expresses Itself in me, with all my lack of respect and charity for those other bloody-handed expressions. I'm sure I'll have to learn to be more charitable.

The Whole Thing is all right. The sense of wonder assures me, more and more. It takes less and less to activate it. The sun in the morning and the moon at night. My companion and her smile. Friends and their encouragement. Birds out back under the walnut tree. A leaf that falls with a clatter, making me notice. Next year's larkspur, already claiming their bit of soil. It is all full of wonder.

A Zen Buddhist master entered the garden of a monastery. He walked over to a statue of the seated Buddha and spat down onto the top of its head. A novice cried out, "How can you spit on the Buddha?"

The master replied, "Tell me, then, where I'm to spit, so's not to spit on the Buddha?"

IV. Living Free

A. What We'll Need

In **Out of the Silent Planet**, by C. S. Lewis, the protagonist, Ransom, is quite impressed, to put it mildly, by the fact that he has journeyed to Mars. But at some point later in the novel, Ransom marvels even more that he has been living for many weeks on Mars.

Breaking free of the God-obsession is a marvelous achievement. But after it's been accomplished, it becomes even more amazing that we can go on, we can actually live, free of that heavy weight that used to drag us down.

You have your life handed to you. The chains are gone, the doors are open, you can breathe and move and decide for yourself. You'll feel light, light-headed, light-hearted. You'll think you're dreaming.

Also, you'll think you just arrived in what feels like a more solid reality. The world you now get to live in and make decisions in is not a flimsy theological house of cards, and not a rigid ecclesiastical prison. Your exhilaration is entirely understandable. You get to live your own life!

Life in the real world, on your own, will require some skills, some talents that you've had latent within you, but which haven't been encouraged much because of the God-

158

obsession. We now need to look at them.

Honesty

The God-obsession can lead to a great deal of debilitating dishonesty. For one thing, self-appraisal is not encouraged. I was told bluntly that I spent too much time and effort in introspection, even though it seemed to me that even more introspection would have been a good idea in my case, and also in the cases of those who were trying to warn me away from it.

If, upon self-examination, you decide you're good, that will be called pride. If you decide that you're bad, you will be agreeing with the old doctrine of sin. But if you decide that you really need to change, that may cause a lot of trouble for those around you, and may suggest that you don't believe in the forgiveness "God" offers. They may tell you plainly that it's really better not to think about it. Blanket statements in creeds and confessions are designed to sweep away any attempt at careful honest self-appraisal.

This leaves out some very important questions. What kind of person am I? What do I want? Am I happy? Is this all there is? Doesn't it seem late? Are we in sudden-death overtime?

God-obsessed people tend to fence off certain areas and forbid questions about them. Sacred cows and axioms — leave them alone. When the wise children ask, "Why?" these persons become nervous. I recall how upset folks became in the old days when I announced that my policy with young people, in youth groups and camps or wherever, was going to be, "No illegal questions." So we talked about war and sex and history and "God," but we were making the God-obsessed people in charge of things very unhappy.

The refusal to look at evidence was an old patterned response. When the cardinals rejected that chance to see the mountains on the moon by looking through Galileo's telescope, they provided us a symbol of the basic dishonesty of their position. Their axiom that the moon was a perfect sphere told them that there couldn't be any mountains on it, so why look? The way theology can attempt to ride roughshod over plain facts should warn a sensitive person, and the clue is simple honesty.

All through seminary I balked at the idea of ordination. I did not believe that clergy were in any way different from the people. I had an extremely egalitarian form of Christianity in my heart. I liked the Quaker system, at least in theory — they had no clergy at all.

There was one little catch. I couldn't go serve the people I felt called to without being ordained. In comparison to my eagerness to go west to a place I had never been, like Abraham, who went out not knowing where he was going, my ecclesiastical doubts about the efficacy of "the laying on of hands" carried little weight. So I underwent the Presbytery examination for ordination.

It was an all-day, formal oral examination, by a committee, mostly of young pastors. I did very well in Bible and church history and "polity," that is, how the Presbyterian Church is organized. The interesting part was theology. I knew the history, the schools, the definitions. I knew Augustine and Calvin and Schopenhauer and Schleiermacher.

When it came to what I personally believed, we hit a snag. I did not believe in the Virgin Birth. I thought it was an anti-woman, anti-sex doctrine, cooked up by frustrated celibates, and that it detracted from the full humanity of Jesus. "Oh, that's what we think, too," one of the examiners said.

"Aha!" said I. "So what should I say when you ask me, in the ordination ceremony, whether I believe that the Westminster Confession of Faith contains *that* system of doctrine taught in the Holy Scriptures?" The Westminster Confession of Faith was written in 1643, as part of the Cromwellian Revolution in England! The ordination questions were meant to cement modern loyalty to that. "I don't believe the Scriptures teach a single system of doctrine at all — the Scriptures are far too complex for that. And just for instance, I don't believe personally in the Doctrine of the Virgin Birth. So, should I say, 'No'?"

They all smiled, looking at each other. "Oh, no, don't do that," one said. "That would stop proceedings." They chuckled.

I didn't see the humor in it at all, then. "I'm to lie?"

"It isn't a lie exactly. We all know what you mean."

"So, I should say, 'Yes,' meaning, 'No.'" They squirmed, knowing perfectly well that I was alluding to one of Jesus' sayings about simple honesty. "Let your 'yes' be 'yes' and your 'no,' 'no.' Anything more than this springs from evil."

They looked sheepish. "We all did it. We're working to change the ordination ceremony. You can help us."

It was subtle. Guys I liked, who wanted to be honest but weren't being so, were encouraging me to join them.

But the only way I could join them was to be as dishonest as they. It was going to be called "boring from within." It was later going to be compared to the French Underground — "Smile at the Nazis all day, and blow 'em up at night."

But, from this perspective, the dishonesty stands out more than anything else. My view of all this would be colored forever by the sense of relief, the freedom I felt, when I could at last, upon quitting and demitting ten years later, be honest again.

Truth is clean and exhilarating, like fresh air for a penned-in spirit. Truth arches over our beliefs, our systems, our excuses, our memories. I am forever grateful to the college professor who challenged me to "follow the truth wherever it leads." If it threatens or contradicts "faith," I found I'd have to go with truth. It was a golden thread guiding me through all those years when I was trying to juggle all this, trying to stay in when much of me wanted out, trying to find additional excuses for myself and others, trying to throttle my own selfhood in the name of commitment and old promises and obedience, trying to squelch doubts and hinder the process of growth that would not stop just because I found it painful. Truth finally had its way. I couldn't lie anymore.

Before the break, I had to pretend to believe what I didn't any longer believe. I had to pretend I didn't feel what I did feel. I had to appear to be on the side of people whose actions were reprehensible and evil. I mean, if they're Christian and I'm Christian, we're Christians together, right? I'm in the same group with the Ku Klux Klan and the Pentagon and the President who bombed

Cambodia and the Pope and the Curia who hinder efforts at population control. I couldn't be honest about where I stood on any of those serious matters.

I tried "boring from within," very deliberately, for several years. I was getting nowhere with my boring, and the dishonesty was killing me. The fetid air was suffocating. I had to get out and breathe the fresh air of truth.

One of the most liberating things was the phrase, "I don't know." For a clergyman the phrase undermines his position entirely. "Why is she dying?" "Why isn't he dying?" "What is God trying to pull here?" "Where is God?" "Is there a God at all, to allow this?" When I answered, "I don't know," great consternation resulted. The prophet/priest doesn't know! The officially-appointed representative of the omniscient God doesn't know!

Later, as a teacher, it liberated the entire class every time I admitted that I didn't know. It had that same odor of a fresh breeze, because it was honest. You don't know? The teacher doesn't know! Aren't the answers in the back of the book? You mean I have to figure it out for myself? And live my life on my own, meanwhile?

I'm not saying honesty is the best policy. I'm not sure of that. We've had politicians and corporate managers who became very powerful and very rich by being very dishonest. They seemed to die happy. Luxury and peace prizes and huge retirement pensions and the adulation of media and crowds came to them from their dishonest behavior. For me, honesty is better because it's more fun, more relaxing. I don't have to remember the daisy-chain of lies, or pay off those who know better. But then, I'm not running for President, or trying to fool all the people all of the time.

I'm left believing that honesty is a good policy, and the best for me. Now I can say openly that I don't believe certain things. I can even say that I know better in some cases. I can say what I feel and admit that maybe shortly that'll change. Now I can remember as accurately as possible, with no need for cover-up.

I think dishonesty spoils one of our special human abilities, that of language. What is language for? We have already noticed that anthropologist who went so far as to propose that the function of language is to lie, to dissimulate, to deceive, to gain additional control over the environment by placing the other nearby humans in error. But I think that's a common and unfortunate corruption of language, not the purpose of it. Its advantage, back when it evolved, was to consolidate co-operation, to sharpen warnings and instructions, to contain memories and provide a vehicle for passing them on.

Language is so corrupted now by dishonesty, at the personal and social and international level, that it's not hard to imagine someone suggesting that lying is what language simply is and all that it is. But language can still be a tool for truth. "This is what I see." "This is what I feel." "This is what I remember." "This is what So-and-so told me." "This is where I found apples." "This roof leaks." "When you subtract a large number from a small number you get a negative number." True statements are still possible. I'm going to remain on the look-out for them, and provide as many of my own as I can. It's a good feeling not to be hampered by the God-obsession.

Just two footnotes on truth. Conventional wisdom says that there are two sides to every question. It's mostly so, but with some important exceptions. The exceptions, for which I have not yet been able to locate the second side, are:

[1] The Environment. If we don't have a live environment, we aren't going to have an economy, or a democratic republic, or any freedom, or any profit.

[2] Nuclear War. If we have a nuclear war, we aren't going to have a live environment, or an economy, or a democratic republic, or any freedom, or any profit.

[3] Overpopulation. If we become so numerous that we can't co-exist on this planet, we aren't going to have a live environment, or an economy, or a democratic republic, or any freedom, or any profit.

If there is a second side to any of these questions, which is not some private greedy, short-lived, arbitrary ducking of the question, I haven't heard it yet. I include theological ducking, such as, "God won't allow such a thing," as one more unsatisfactory attempt to make an argument without a case.

But let's get back to our little private lives, where the indignation about these planetary issues must find its source. The most deadly dishonesty is self-deception. If you fool yourself into thinking you believe the absurd or the illogical, if you fool yourself into saying you don't feel what you feel, you'll be in trouble. You'll be susceptible to being lied to by politicians and preachers. And you'll delay getting your life in order and getting on with it.

"To thine own self be true." If not, who are you

kidding? Adam and Jonah tried to hide from God. They're good stories — excellent metaphors. You can't hide from yourself, from the Self. You can't hide from Reality. Enjoy giving up trying. Enjoy the relief.

Courage

It takes courage to wake up in the morning and find that you're still you, and then get up and wash your face and go have at another day. It takes courage to grow old, and to be old. It takes courage to breathe, knowing the air is poisonous, to drink water not knowing what's in it, to go out in traffic driving or walking, to greet a stranger with a smile. It takes courage to examine your life in the silence of your lonely room and take responsibility for it.

Life is a journey. Life is a one-way road. We're not sure where we're going. I say flatly that those who are sure are in error. Being a sensitive and aware human being is a stint full of pain and loneliness. Memories add to the pain, sometimes. We're sorry it happened the way it did. Or we're sorry those times are gone forever. We miss old companions. Some of them were a little like toothache, and we miss them all right, but others were like a piece of our very selves, now gone.

The journey is lonely, at least at times. The search for honesty, for self-respect, for a life free of the God-obsession and any other inherited disabilities alienates the Searcher from other people.

"You think of the damnedest things!" "Why worry about that?" "There's nothing you can do about that." "You think too much." "Too much introspection is bad for you." "Everyone compromises all the time." "Everyone has his price." "There are two sides to everything." "Take it easy." "Quit worrying about it." "Don't take it so hard." "Don't make such a thing out of it." "Cool it."

In my case, such advice from Job's comforters, family mostly, called into question my mental health and stability. "Your ideas are wild and insane." "You're crazy." "You're nuts." Harry is nuts. Harry has a screw loose. Harry is bananas. Harry has slipped his trolley. Harry doesn't have all his buttons. The lights are on, but nobody's home.

Actually, that last statement did describe pretty well what I have to call my zombie period. But the rest of the comments were simply untrue, flippant attempts to put me into some kind of category which people could handle without joining me in thought.

I was going sane, but people called it the opposite. "Well, what are we to think? This nice young man, this plain-looking, unrobed clergyman, leaves his church, begins to dress in bright colors, becomes involved in all-night encounter group marathons, goes into dream therapy, pretends he's a black man or a brown one, gets a divorce, remarries, acts like he's trying to enjoy life instead of being the sober, serious, irrelevant clergyman we always wanted — he's flipped his lid! He's gone ape! He's crazy!"

It takes courage to find real friends and fellow-searchers, beyond the group of compulsory fellow-members. It takes effort, too. It takes courage to reclassify your long-held axiomatic beliefs as "false," "uncertain," "unlikely," "unnecessary", or "true, after all." It takes courage to change your life, your work, your intentions, your goals, your daily routine, your circle of companions. And it takes courage to persist in your search.

There is a danger for people who get rid of the God-obsession. It is the danger of stopping in mid-process, in disbelief and bitter anger. Jesus told a story about that. A man had a devil cast out of him. The devil went and found seven other devils worse than himself and came back and found the man empty. So all the devils entered into him, and, as Jesus put it, "the last state of that man was worse than the first." Stopping in mid-process is what that story is really all about. Don't be content just to get rid of the old error. Go on to find what you discover to be Truth.

You'll feel anger at the half-way point. People took advantage of you when you were little, fed you a lot of crap, lied to you, expected you to behave in ways that throttled your talents and your chances, and many other and worse things happened to you as victim. You'll stir up plenty of fury as you piece together your own story.

You'll be tempted to throw out everything. Not only God and Creator and Savior and priest and church and prophecy and tithing and offerings and meaningless ritual observations, but also peace and love and justice and joy and truth and patience and some other good things. That's the dangerous period. We call it, "throwing out the baby with the bath." The question is, "What is the baby?" False ideas about God, or God, or something else? Bad experiences with church people, or church? Bad motives on my part and traitors in the midst, or the cause of peace and justice? An infantile mixture of need and anger and frustration, or love? Each one will have to continue to work on all that. I know I do. My main concern is that we finish this process. The danger is out there in the middle.

The only way out is through. Finish determining what you want, what you want to be, what you're going to base your life on. Don't flounder and drift and let what comes be by default. Christianity and the God-obsession provide too-easy and too-glib answers to some questions that have a way of hanging around. Life itself has a way of forcing us to pay attention.

Chesterton said, "Christianity has not failed. It has never been tried." If he's allowed to define his own terms, he's no doubt right. I suppose he means that Christianity is not the Vatican or the Crusades or the World Council of Churches or tax-exemptions or the good-guys in the struggle against atheistic materialistic communism. It's loving yourself and your neighbor and your enemy and working to build a just society which includes the whole world. If so, it hasn't yet been tried, indeed.

My own notion is this: Christianity is the type of belief, which, the more seriously you take it, the more surely you'll outgrow it. I consider myself, not an ex-Christian, thrown out or back-slid, as if I'd forgotten some verse and could be reclaimed, if only I'd recollect it all aright and "go home to Mamma," meaning Holy Mother Church. No, I'm a post-Christian. I did that. I tried that. I gave that the best try I could — and went right on through, right on past that safe haven, that shrine dedicated to unchangeable cosmic security which is a kind of inner death — and here I am out in the sunshine and fresh air, free on a planet that I'm a native of, pondering a Cosmos that beckons to me and persuades me to be in awe, plunked down in the middle of a world full of people to love and share with.

Old habits, old patterns — I find they're not all bad, after all. The notion that I'm here to do my best, with no shirking, persists. The notion persists that my life, my talents, my unique experiences, my intelligence, the energy that flows through me — all that is a gift I hold in stewardship. The old notion persists that knowing the truth can set a body free. The old dream persists that all of us are here to love and care for and enjoy each other.

Imagination

Imagination is a skill that can be very helpful on the journey of life. All humans have the inclination and the ability, but some of us who were raised in the middle of the God-obsession found it squelched for a while. Our imaginary stories were all prescribed — Bible myths and nonsense tales like "The Three Little Pigs." Personally made-up imaginary mental meanderings were shushed as foolish, or "thinking too much, once again," or a form of "lying." It seemed clear to the adults that what one makes up in his own head isn't truth. So, what is it?

Now that we're out here in the fresh air, we discover that we need the ability to develop the imagination. It's our creativity, and we're allowed full use of it. There are two main areas where you'll find that you need it.

The first is in preparing a script of your own for your life. After half a life-time of following prepackaged scripts written by other people, you find yourself "on your own." This may be scary. Some can't handle it and scurry back to "bondage." It would be worth it to read Exodus and Numbers again, skipping the non-narrative sections. Watch the unimaginative Israelites resist and resent the responsibilities and the exhilarating possibilities of freedom.

"Oh, that we had meat to eat! We remember the fish we ate in Egypt for nothing, the cucumbers, the melons, the leeks, the onions, and the garlic; but now our strength is dried up, and there is nothing at all but this manna to look at." They didn't like miracle-food, and they pretended that slaves eat "for nothing." But fear, and a lack of imagination, can cause that kind of crazy dishonesty.

Imagination will help you stay free. "What shall I do? What are the rules?" you ask. There are none you dare not examine and evaluate!

"What if I do such-and-such?" you ask. Let's see. Follow it for a while, in your mind. Imagine. Visualize.

"Could I do this, or that?" you ask. Why not? Are you asking about ability, or power, or permission? You have permission!

"What will be the consequences?" you well may ask. There's no telling, for sure, but you certainly may try your imagination.

Let your imagination run. Let it take off and fly. Liberate it. The old patterns and the old habits will hedge it in plenty, in spite of your new resolve to be a free agent in this world, but keep at it. Let it be your new Quiet Time. "What are you doing?" someone will ask you.

"Imagining," tell them. "Dreaming!" And that'll be all to the good.

The other main arena for your imagination will be in trying on other people's moccasins. We all need to do a lot of it. I was lucky in this. As a fairly young adult I ended up in Spain with wife and kids, and the assignment of learning Spanish within a year. I did it, and it changed my thought-processes. It enlarged my head somehow. The experience doubled the number of nerve-endings. It gave me another tool with which to think and categorize what I saw and heard. I had new thoughts to think, and new untranslatable kinds of awareness. It changed me permanently. I highly recommend the learning of a second language, not an hour a week or an hour a day, but total immersion until the second language really is learned. Drop the natural habitual question, "Why do they say that?" Replace it with, "What are they saying? And what do they mean by what I just heard?"

Anyway, I learned to think like a Spaniard. I became a kind of Johnny-come-lately Spaniard. I spent a great deal of effort learning to sound and think and react like a Spaniard. It did me a world of good. Our white American way of thinking is not the correct way — it is just one of many ways.

We all need to use our imagination to the full, in order to understand each other. What's it like to be black? I spent enough time in Atlanta working for Martin Luther King's Southern Christian Leadership Conference that I caught myself reacting to strangers on Auburn Avenue at night as if I were black. "Oh, he's a brother..." meaning, "I see a black face." The fact that my face was still white was something of a complication, and maybe a little scary for the oncoming brother, but at least in my mind my own whiteness had been left behind momentarily.

What's it like to be brown? I was so intent on finding out I married her. I'm still working on it.

What's it like to be a native of the Western Hemisphere, not from India, living in poverty because everything has been stolen, regarded as a tourist attraction, which is only slightly better than being regarded as a dangerous wild animal? I have long had this feeling that I was a Susquehannock, long ago, in another life, but that's pretty far out. That notion became part of the plot of a novel of mine: **Souls and Cells Remember: a Love Story**.

What's it like to be a scared, arrogant, rigid, friendly, contradictory, skinny little white missionary? No fun, mostly, as I remember it.

What's it like to be a teacher who knows, let's say, 1.23% of the sum total of what there is to be known, and thinks he has to pound that same 1.23% into his students' heads? My theoretical estimate of how much any one person can know in this day and age is far too high, but the question is really meant to mock the teacher's arrogance. I have been there.

What's it like to be a heretic? Dangerous, lonely, exciting. I know about that one.

What's it like to be a male WASP? I have trouble with it, frankly, because I know. Pogo let the truth escape: "We have met the enemy, and he is us."

What's it like to hide in a hole while your bamboo house is being burned to the ground and your teenagers are out fighting, killing and being killed? Try to imagine.

What's it like to be a woman? Something deep inside

me knows a little about that already, perhaps a lot. Half of the world already knows from current experience, and we'll all benefit, when they take over more areas and then ask, "What's it like to be a male?"

What's it like to be a scoundrel who must lie with every breath because of all the previous lies told already? Imagine, imagine.

What was it like to be my father? I'm not sure — I saw all that from my end of it only, beginning in what was already the middle of the story. I also missed a great deal of the last parts of the story, too — but I am a father myself, so perhaps I can imagine... a little.

What's it like to be my son? I'm not sure — I saw all that from my end only, and I was busy with that obsession and other things at the same time, and I'm missing most of the current portion of the story — but I am a son myself, so I can imagine, a little.

Imagination will take us a long way toward awareness and sensitivity and understanding. Sometimes we humans feel like an unrelated heap of scattered lonely and all-too-hostile parts. Reunifying them is what the alchemists called The Great Work, which is going on all around us all the time. We can join in the process. I'm not referring to the attempt to melt everything and everyone down into identical replaceable parts. That's going on, too, but I think we should resist that. I'm talking about making connections.

Each is special, including you. Each has a uniqueness that is irreplaceable. We don't need to erase all those differences. We need to affirm them, value them, understand them, and embrace them and allow them to enrich the whole.

Use your imagination to make of yourself the most interesting and self-aware and unusual and special person you can be. And use your imagination to connect yourself to all these other marvelously fascinating people.

Humor

One of the most liberating gifts you have is your ability to laugh at yourself. If you can't do that, if you can't see, or can't let yourself admit that you see, that you're a pretentious bag of wind, some of the time, that you take yourself more seriously than the overall facts can possibly justify, that you insist on pretending that your view of things is the only correct one, then you may be stuck for a while yet. When it all strikes you as somehow, well, comical, then the thing will be going into motion. Hang on, because then the fun begins.

Our lives are a series of absurd pretensions. We do bizarre and funny things to get ahead, to amount to something, to keep up pretenses, to hide our bodily functions, to hide our ignorance, to preserve our cardboard reputations. All we have to do is admit that, to ourselves first of all, and then the process of liberation is well under way.

God-obsessed people have extra pretensions to be unnecessarily sober and serious about. Sex is mixed up in all this somehow, and so is money. And since no one really, really has given up very much concern about either thing, the pretensions have become hilarious. "Money is evil," we were taught, but you can't live without a fairly steady supply. "Sex is evil," they told us, but the species can't survive without it and the glands are unmanageable, no matter who says what.

Incongruity is one of the main roots of humor. A good laugh can blow away the basic contradictions so many of us have tried to live by.

In my case ordination to the clergy was the greatest pretense, and is now the greatest source of mirth. "On Being a Deity," I have come to call it. I knew better, but I allowed it anyway. Now a good bit of the humor can be sensed in the no longer quite so painful memory of the discomfiture I felt every time I received the deity treatment, and in our shared wonderment at how long I allowed it.

Clergy/deities are pure, everyone assumed. They have no hormones, they deserve special discounts, they are non-physical and thus do not need food, their children are immaculately conceived, their prayers are more effective than those of ordinary mortals, and they can handle all the hostility that is intended for God Himself. It is all extremely funny now.

It wasn't always. Once, as a very young deity, I was sent to a certain lady at the behest of her sister-in-law. After a little observation, I suggested to her that maybe she could perhaps think about maybe considering maybe the possibility of her getting some — uh, well, professional psychological help. Her scream pierced my skull like a flaming arrow and peeled paint off the wall behind me. "I AM NOT NUTS!!" I ran like a rabbit.

On another occasion I overheard two young boys' banter as they played catch. "Holy Shit!" cried one, as the ball stung in his glove.

"Preacher's is," the other said.

"Ha-ha," they both said. I scratched my head in wonder. Then I had to grin, because this preacher knew better.

Someone asked my six-year-old what he wanted to be when he grew up. "A preacher."

"Why?"

"So I can scream at people." Laugh, laugh. It wasn't really very funny then, but we laughed. It still isn't, really, but we chuckle, remembering.

Near the end of the deity period, I was asked by a dear friend, an unordained missionary to a nearby Indian pueblo, to come to a special evening service and baptize some infants. He didn't dare baptize them, since he wasn't an ordained, card-carrying deity. I had never believed in infant baptism, but did it from time to time rather than create useless fuss. I consented this time for my friend's sake, and because of a kind of curiosity on my part about Indian rituals. Maybe I could learn something.

When we arrived, there was no drumming and no dancing and no special clothing. It was a tiny group of plain people, in a bare Protestant chapel, with no special rituals and no symbolism of any kind. There were two candidates for infant baptism, but one was no longer a babe in arms. He was afoot and restless, trotting around and singing.

At the appropriate time in the ceremony I asked the mother, "What is the Christian name of this child?"

"Shadrach Moses."

I wished I had asked in advance, so that I could have

had a more private reaction to the name itself. Shadrach
Moses. Yes. Two great ones. But a modern-day Pueblo
Indian with that name? I was full of laugh and full of
admiration for the courage to select such a name. I
squatted down to confront him, as he clutched his
mother's skirt. She was holding his infant brother in her
arms.

My friend reached down with a glass bowl full of
water, which we had prayed over according to proper
rituals. I dipped my hand in and lifted as much water as
would stay between my fingers. I slapped this wetness
gently on the little boy's head and said, "Shadrach Moses,
I baptize thee —"

He bolted with a wild yell, ducking out from under me
and the magic water, scooted around his mother and ran
pell-mell the short distance to the door and out into the
black dark night. He was gone, gone out into the dark
mysterious pueblo. "— in the name of the Father, and of
the Son, and of the Holy Spirit. Amen." It sounded like
an afterthought. I stood up. The mother stared at me
wordlessly from her huge round eyes. She jiggled slightly
the baby in her arms. A man left the room and also
disappeared into the night.

"What is the Christian name of this child?"

"Benjamin Michael."

Benjamin Michael screamed while I wet his head, but
my mind was on Shadrach Moses. Big white medicine
man scared the pie outa him. Did his grandfather find
him? What's he thinking? What are we doing? What is
going on? I chuckle every time I remember it. Shadrach
Moses avoided me, when his grandfather did bring him

back, after our little service was concluded. I regret that
I haven't seen him again since that night, and haven't been
able to find him. I tell it to share the humor that has
replaced the indignation and humiliation that I felt for a
while, when I recalled that I had allowed people to make
me into a sort of deity.

In all my study of mythology, which ranged far and
wide in my effort to put myself together after all that fell
apart, I came upon the Tarot cards. One of them is called
The Devil. And one of the occult meanings of that card,
I learned, is Mirth.

It depicts a horrible monster, with the horns and ears
of a goat, the face of a jackass, the glowing red eyes of a
demon, the wings of a huge bat, the shoulders and arms
of a Pittsburgh Steeler, the legs and feet of some bird like
a rooster. He's sitting on a half-cube.

Chained to the cube are two naked human figures, one
male and one female, good-looking, well-built, except
they have horns and hooves and tails. Her tail is like a
huge raspberry fruit on the end of a green stem. His tail
is a large flame at the end of a fiery yellow stem.

Here we are, bestialized, chained to an imaginary
bogeyman. But if you look carefully, you notice that the
chains around our necks are loose. We may remove them,
when we wish. We are chained to this non-existent devil,
as long as we choose to be. We volunteer to stay.

Clarity about all this is cause for mirth. Freedom is
ready and waiting, whenever we decide we want it. And
after we lift our chains off, we'll look back and see what
comical fools we made of ourselves, and we'll laugh.

And here comes the best joke of all. After making such

fun of myself and all the people who helped perpetuate the absurd fiction of my being a deity, I find it's true. I am IT. I am an expression of The All. So are you. And so are all of them.

You are IT.

You are the Pearl of Great Price. Don't let anything get in the way of your finding it. Don't lose it. Don't throw it away.

You are the treasure hidden in the field. Do whatever it takes to make sure it's found.

You are the light of the world. Let it shine, let it shine, let it shine.

You are IT!

You are a creative artist, and the most important artistic undertaking of any human being is one's own life.

Love

Recall the statement from one of the God-is-dead theologians of the 1960s: "The faith is flawed. The love is not."

My main quarrel with fundamentalist, right-wing, conservative Christianity, which is so much in vogue these days, is that it is mean-hearted. The theology is nasty. It provides a literal hell of eternal conscious torment for the majority of our species. It condemns to death and hell innocent babies who have the bad luck of being born under communist regimes, or in societies untouched by missionaries. The God of this group is a secret weapon used to attack all who disagree with their own narrow hate-filled beliefs.

Spokesmen for that theology are quick to label as "sin, condemned by God," what other thoughtful persons would be willing to call tragedy or perfectly legitimate variety — such things as abortion and homosexuality. They are unsympathetic toward the poor and helpless. They favor the death penalty. They are more ready to spend money on prisons than on nutrition, and far more on war than on education and cultural exchange. The God/idol they worship is cruel and mean, because they are.

I said all that in the presence of a woman whose teen-age son had recently become caught up in one of the many thriving right-wing fundamentalist groups for college students. "I don't think there's a mean bone in his body," she protested.

"Then he'll outgrow it," I replied, confident of the truth of it, remembering my own case. He won't be able to stomach the unrelenting smugness and nastiness.

Martin Luther spotted this clue, back in the sixteenth century. "If the Pope really does have the power and authority to release souls from Purgatory, then *why doesn't he, for love's sake?"* He was exposing an unloving theology.

"Love never fails." It's a sweeping statement from the greatest theological sweeping-statement-maker of them all, the Apostle Paul. Sometimes he's right, though, perhaps by accident. This time he's right, because love is built into the Way-It-Is. That being so, it is universal, and thus for everybody.

I studied and pondered all this long ago in university science classes, first chemistry and then biology. I didn't realize then exactly what I was studying — the evidence that love is at the root of all that exists. We have noted already that the Cosmos is stirred by something I called Desire. Let's look again.

Take chemistry. Consider the valance bond. Certain atoms are attracted to each other. The metals are those that have one or two extra electrons spinning around beyond the last outer ring. It amounts to a projection which the atom is inclined to get rid of. The atom "wants" to be rid of those electrons. Sure, I'm using a metaphor. A sodium atom doesn't really "want" to get rid of something, like a horny college sophomore, right? And who else would notice the metaphor?

Another group of atoms "wants" to complete the outer ring of electrons. Usually eight completes it, but some have only six or seven. They have a gap they want filled. The focal point of the attraction is a space, where something is needed to fulfill it. Sure, it's a metaphor! But what's going on at the level of atoms and molecules and chemical bonds and ionization and the formation of chemical compounds looks suspiciously like sex to me. That attraction, that desire to combine, to be rid of the extra, to find the needed additional — it's in the atoms. Projections and gaps — and completion by unification. Yes, it's a metaphor.

Take biology. The professor went to great lengths to show how, over eons, life forms change and evolve — from simple chordates to cartilaginous fishes to bony fishes to amphibians and then reptiles and then birds and mammals, in all their variety. We were doing vertebrate anatomy only, so plants and insects and worms and microbes were left out of his story. But it was enough —

all that gradual development over all those hundreds of millions of years.

One of the students exclaimed, "God, that was a lot of copulating!" Actually he used the Anglo-saxon word. The other students chortled, and the professor couldn't hide the slightest grin — he was the same one who had challenged me about Truth.

I pondered it all. The skinny little future missionary had to translate it into Latin in order to think about it, in those days. "Yes. It was a lot of copulating! To bring that about. The toads and the dinosaurs and the eagles and the chickens and the tigers and the monkeys and pithecanthropus erectus — what a lot of copulating! That's mostly what was going on! For hundreds of millions of years!"

Chemistry and biology told it plainly enough. There is an attraction. A yearning for unity, which produces something new as it achieves its desire.

Can we call that love? Why not? Many excellent books have been written about love. Fromm's **The Art of Loving** and C. S. Lewis' **The Four Loves** are basic. They tell all about all the different kinds of love. I'm trying to get at what's common to them all — and it's the tendency toward union, or reunion.

The Greeks had three words, all of which we translate "love." *Philos* is between friends. It's a little abstract, as in "philanthropy" or "philosophy." It's a pale kind of love, with a minimum of gutsy commitment and no passion.

Agape is the New Testament word for the love of God. "God's unmerited favor." Whenever I try to feel it or express it, it comes out containing pity, and I detect a

streak of despising in it. "I can't hate him. I feel sorry for
him. I wish him well — and hope deep down in here to
have little or no further contact with or news about or
interference from him." When it's pity, love is flawed.

Eros is the word for love. I'm not sure there's any love
that doesn't have *Eros* in it. *Eros* is what the atoms are
doing, and the life forms on Planet Earth. *Eros* is
affirming the good in the other, and wanting contact and
union. It can become fouled up, at least among humans,
to be sure. Sometimes it is mixed with aggressiveness and
becomes predatory. It seems to remain purer among the
animals. The tiger doesn't love the sambur — he eats it.
The male tiger loves, in some sense, the female tiger and
copulates with her, when she's ready.

Eros makes the world go round. It is a little scary for
us formerly hemmed-in God-obsessed people. In order to
overcome that fear, I recommend a good dose of
sensuality to arouse *Eros* and keep it awake. Absorb the
whole world through your senses. See more. See it all.
Hear it all. Touch and feel. Taste and smell. Try painting,
music, flowers, nudity, bubble baths. Be beautiful. Smile.
Flirt. Allow your glands to function.

Twice I've been saved by the glands. The first time, it
was from an icy mechanical inhuman arrogance. I didn't
realize what a fiendish self-winding studying machine I
had become in my prideful service to the Lord. She came
along, unasked for, and seemed to like me, which was
unusual. She smiled, wrinkled her nose, got close — and,
Pow! — the poor little would-be medical missionary was
knocked off his track. Dragged out of himself. Interested
in someone else! Ready to give and sacrifice and risk

everything and change everything and take on the almighty Will of God, no less — in order to have her. Sure, it was sex. It was love, too, and it saved me from a juiceless, tasteless, rigid, frigid fate worse than death.

The second time the glands saved me from despair. Failure made me fearful. I turned the power way down low, one notch from "Off." I became a zombie, a feelingless dead man. And then I saw her. In my own backyard. She was there all the time. And she loved me, had loved me for ages. She wanted me, this human derelict. She was willing to risk it all for me. I came to life, startling everybody. The only other sign of life for some while had been sporadic outbursts of anger, like twitches from a dying nervous system. All that melted away. He became certifiably twitterpated, and life began anew. He was blind, and now could see. He was dead, and is alive again.

I don't think it would have happened without the glands, in either case. I had to give in to Desire. And what is Desire? Desire is IT, The-Whole-Thing, intending something.

I learned some things that have been of value since:

[1] I am not a "good" person. All the rules, all the attempts to be a model for others, all the pretence at "righteousness" — what a word! — were blown away when Desire roused her gorgeous self. Both times.

[2] I am a vehicle of a very powerful Drive. Nothing less than IT, that drives the atoms and the life forms, drives me. This vehicle doesn't drive itself — not when we're really getting somewhere.

[3] I am an agent of the Life Force. Yes, I said that

already, but it's nothing short of amazing, nevertheless.

[4] I must let go of myself. My "ego" doesn't like it — ecstasy, I mean. So it's good-bye ego, since I like ecstasy.

[5] My "ego" cannot protect itself with rules. And it wasn't worth the trouble anyway. The attempt simply delayed getting "with it." "The only thing that we done wrong, was stayin' in the wilderness too long. Keep your eye on the prize."

[6] I am free to love. I dare to love myself, at last. Then I find I love the Self, in all its expressions. I love the Other, with all that built-in attraction and attractiveness. Promiscuity is not the result, not at all. Union is the result. And the freedom to be pleasant, friendly, open, caring, relaxed, helpful even, not concerned about "where this relationship is going."

So love remains. Here's a proverb that should be added to The Book. "'Tis better to have loved and lost, than never to have loved at all." If you lose, you're losing ego, and that's good for you, painful as it is. What you gain by loving is participation in what IT is doing.

B. What to Do with Ego

The ego is what the sense of humor laughs at, whether that sense is aimed inward or outward. The healthy sense of humor notes how ridiculous one's own ego is. And the pretensions of those other, often threatening, egos that surround a person, make for the jokes of the world, practical and otherwise.

On the other hand, when we see The Self looking out at us from inside the face of the other, we do not joke. We clasp hands in front of our chests, and bow very slightly, and smile just a little.

But the ego is always fair game, mine or yours or anybody's. Ego is Greek, and Latin, for "I." Ego is what we unthinkingly refer to when we say, "I." It takes some years to build an ego. An infant doesn't seem to have one — he thinks he himself is the whole world. But then things gradually separate out, and the child becomes aware of himself as a separate entity in the midst of many.

Four elements constitute the root of the sense of personal identity in the minds of most people in our culture.

[1] Memory
[2] Separateness
[3] Unity of Essence
[4] A Responsible Center

187

[1] Memory. I am I, because I remember being the same person I was before. I'm the one who did that, and that and that. I go to sleep at night, and wake up in the morning, and there I am, the same one who went to sleep earlier. "Oh, it's you again," I sometimes say to myself. I'm the one who did that, and that, and promised to do that, and that. I ate that dinner, I read that book, I wrote that essay, I caned that chair.

Memory is tricky, however. Some of us try to remember especially those things that make us look good. We want to exalt, or exonerate, or elevate, or excuse ourselves, or improve on the high opinion we hope other folks have of us. What other people think figures very highly in the sense of ego. Sometimes it consists of little more than what we hope other people are thinking of us.

Others of us, those with a markedly low opinion of ourselves, tend to remember the bad things and end up feeling guilt and shame and remorse and inadequacy and ineptitude. "I blew that one, and I'll probably blow this next one, too," we think to ourselves. "No wonder nobody likes me or wants me around." When ego is in that state, one is in trouble.

But memory itself is not as dependable as we tend to think. I have discovered by experience that the more I try to pin down what really happened and what caused what I really felt, especially long ago, the less certain I am that I am remembering it exactly right. And yet I believe that it would be best, if we could remember correctly, and I mean ruthlessly accurately, the good and the bad and the indifferent — all of it. Still, the point being made here is that all of that which one digs up and sorts through isn't one's real self — it's one's memory.

[2] Separation. I am I — not some other person. I am separate from all the others, distinct. I am not an appendage of my parents. I am different from my siblings and my peers. I am an individual, unique and special.

Mass culture, with its emphasis on fads and fashions in consumption and in belief systems, has weakened this sense of separateness. Or rather, mass culture has made the individual feel weak, insecure, and insignificant without the approval and company of the group, that is, without the products which those who pay for mass culture are selling. Many people nowadays have a sense of being one of a huge number of identical and helpless victims, rather than separate and distinct viable, capable individual entities.

At the opposite end of this process is the self-aware one who seems to be turning into a monomaniac. Who does he think he is? How can he pretend not to need anyone else? He pretends not be a part of that huge amorphous mass which makes up humanity. He's so separate, so aware of his separateness and his specialness, he must be crazy.

[3] Unity. Most moderately healthy people think that there is only one of them, one essence deep in there. Multiple personality, which does exist, is regarded as a serious disorder. For most of us, we remain aware that all the roles we have played, all the masks we have put on, all the inner conversations we have had with all the various parts of ourselves, all the past deeds, all the triumphs and failures have been perpetrated or performed or suffered by one entity — me. I did it. I did it all. Or it

was done to me.

[4] Responsibility. I did it. I take the credit and the consequences. I said I'd do it, so I'll do it. If I don't do it, someone else will, or no one else will. Either way, I'm responsible.

This can be a great burden. Some have more of it to carry than others. Only sociopaths have none. I have these duties, these obligations, these debts, these promises to fulfill, these relationships to keep up. To have a friend, I must be a friend. To be a good neighbor means that I have these obligations. To be a citizen, I have privileges and duties.

A part of us is inclined to rebel, some more than others. Why me? Why me and not him? Why must I do that? Who says so? Where did this compulsion come from? What drives me? Good health? Her bad health excuses her, right? Well, I'm tired. What if I quit? I may just quit, if we're not careful.

Then who will do it? And what will that make me — a quitter? A loser? A failure? Round and round we go with our sense of being a responsible center of deliberate action — like a cat chasing its own tail.

Sometimes it is barely conscious. At times it's little more than a dull feeling that I have to get up and go do that again. It doesn't matter what it is that needs doing. Today I have to go see So-and-so. Today I have to go do such-and-such.

When one begins to ponder it, it seems rather miserable, mostly, somehow, this being, or having, an ego. It is something of a problem.

I recall a Big Little Book from my childhood. The

title is not in my memory, where I can get at it just now, but it was about a tiny little boy, about three inches tall, who found a robot in the shape of, and about the size of, a man. It was an iron, mechanical man. Our hero climbed inside its head. There was a hollow space there, like a master control room, with buttons to push and levers to move. The buttons and levers enabled the boy to move the iron robot around and make it do things. This one moves his right arm in that direction. These two, worked together just so, make him walk, with a dangerous lurch at first, but it became smoother with practice.

The Little Robot Soul Boy rode around inside the robot, inside the thing's head. I see it now as a metaphor for the ego, or perhaps the "soul."

Many people think of the ego, and perhaps of the soul, as an entity, like the little three-inch boy who rides inside the robot. This thing is trapped inside the body, rides around inside it, animating it, moving it, guiding it, motivating it. "The spirit is willing but the flesh is weak." "I'm tired, but I'm forcing my body to do more." "My body is giving out." We need to see clearly that it is a metaphor, and not something really there.

The metaphor becomes stronger as we age, unless we think about it. The body weakens — the iron robot rusts, wears thin, wears out. And the ego, the sense of I, which is not weakening at the same rate, wonders how to get the body to obey. It is a fairly serious problem, common to those who are having difficulty aging gracefully. "Screw the golden years," one can hear, more and more often, as we proceed.

The opposite case happens sometimes, too. The mind,

the ego, the little boy inside the robot's head, fades away, fades utterly away completely sometimes, and the body keeps on going on. From my angle of vision, it is a far worse catastrophe than the opposite case. Will the Golden Years never come to an end?

Alan Watts wrote a book, which was very liberating for me, decades ago, and more and more so lately. It was called simply, **The Book**. The subtitle gave it away, **The Secret of Knowing Who You Really Are**. The gist of it was that the ego, which we go to such pains to construct throughout childhood and adolescence, and which takes us through the productive middle years of life, is a metaphor, a thing we invent, a thing which isn't really there at all. The second half of life will be better spent learning how to identify with ego less, get along without it more and more, and prepare for discarding it altogether.

The ego isn't there. It's a conventional way of thinking about the fact that this separate self-aware body has a life to live. But it doesn't correspond to an entity that really does ride around inside the body operating it. That's a metaphor.

The ego-idea is full of paradox. Notice that a big ego, as the phrase is used, means really a weak ego. "What a big ego!" we say, meaning, "Who does he think he is?! He's extremely insecure! He thinks his fecal matter isn't odoriferous! Such a fragile little ego!" We mean that he doesn't know who he is, or what he is, he doesn't have a good grasp of reality as it pertains to him, and he is totally unaware of how he comes across to others.

Likewise, in other situations, we watch the person with a healthy ego and note that it hardly intrudes at all, it's almost as though it wasn't there. That's the original meaning of the word "meek." Not weak, not afraid, but all to the contrary. So sure of himself, deep down in there, that he doesn't need to push himself, make demands, or be the center of attention, because he already has a good healthy sense of who he is.

We get early clues about this task of transcending ego. Ego vanishes in the sleep of night. Ego is no longer driving when we're deep in a day-dream. Ego isn't there where we lose ourselves in total rapt attention, when we're totally engrossed in our work, or our play, or anything interesting. Ego is gone in the midst of the deepest ecstatic orgasm. There are clues!

But ego doesn't like ecstasy. Ego doesn't trust altered states of consciousness. Ego wants to be in total control, even though such a task is hopelessly impossible.

Ego has trouble accepting our mortality. I am coming to believe that all the fretting by philosophers and others about the immortality of the soul, and the resurrection of the body and all that, is pure ego, and that we should be working on getting past that concern.

We'll find out, when we die, won't we? Either we will be permanently asleep — which is no hardship, when you're exhausted — or we awaken to something. We can be curious to see what, and then we'll have to proceed to make the best of it.

Meanwhile, our mortality is what makes life precious. A wife. A friend. The sun, the moon, rain, blue sky. The voice of someone you care about. A smile, meant just for you. None of these things would mean much, if we were eternal, that is, if we were what most people erroneously mean by eternal, which is "without end."

We end. Everything precious to us will end. It is incorrect and immoral to suggest that there is a way to live life so that one can escape mortality. "So-and-so shall never die" is a falsehood.

One of the greatest tragedies that looms as a possibility, given our mortality, is that of the unlived life — good intentions, grandiose plans, little ventured nothing gained, experience avoided, chronic fearfulness, especially fear of some sort of cosmic disapproval — all that can result in the tragedy that I regard as most dire. Had a life and didn't live it.

Because of a growing awareness of my mortality, I am trying to fill my life in such a way that when I die, it will not appear to anyone that I neglected to live. The way to prepare for Death is to pack in a great deal of living.

Certainty about what happens to us when we die is not available. The body disintegrates over time. I am not sure what is meant exactly by "soul" or "spirit," although I do feel that I am somehow not quite exactly merely the same as my body, not merely the body. I have had hints of having lived before, but not quite enough to allow me to make flat statements about reincarnation, or what it is that could have lived in another body at another time or on another plane. But I have had hints. I also have a vivid imagination, which may be all that is required to account for those hints.

I believe that some, but not all, of the pain and trouble we experience in life is self-inflicted. I suspect that most of the difficulty some have in dying is self-inflicted. I believe that we could learn how to die, that in the long run we will learn it, and that that is exactly what we who have lived this long are in the middle of learning.

Remember, Ego is a fiction. The conscious center of awareness, the "I," isn't really there as an entity, but is a convention, a mental trick we play on ourselves in collusion with others. "This dream we all share, which we call Reality" is a way of putting it, and all egos are merely players, roles, characters in the Dream.

Our mortality is a threat to ego. It's a threat to the body, also, but bodies this old are well aware of that, whereas not all egos are capable of admitting it. Life's task, at this stage, is to prepare the ego for its own non-existence.

For some, this is a hard saying. For others — and I am one of them — it sounds like a call home, a call from a far country. The heavy burden, which needs to be laid down at last, is not sin, in spite of what old stories and songs and books declare. It is ego.

I am concluding that Death cannot be accepted by an ego. To the extent that a human being is an ego, it cannot accept, can hardly face at all, the prospect of personal non-existence. Humans with crushed egos can do better — they care nothing about their lives. The danger is, they don't care about anyone else's life either. When people conclude that life is not worth the trouble, I regret that they have missed the joy of it.

Ego doesn't like to think about death. Ego cannot imagine its own annihilation. Most humans try to put out of mind such morbid considerations. We seek protection from the Dread that comes in the night as we unavoidably find ourselves contemplating the real situation, namely that we are doomed. Dread leaks into our consciousness in spite of all our efforts. We are especially vulnerable when we're awake in bed in dark of night.

We can be heard to whimper. And sometimes even those who pretend to be most stalwart and most "realistic," as they like to call it, can be heard to whimper. The entropy theory of the future of the cosmos is a well-known case in point. They are doomed, these individual experts and theorists, and so they infer that The Whole Thing is likewise, that it will be reduced to random uniform virtual non-movement of particles, that The Whole Thing will turn into nothing-at-all.

Yet there is plenty of evidence to the contrary. The birth of new stars, now detectable, and the cyclical nature of all phenomena, are important examples. The entropy theorists leap from their chagrin about their own mortality to a belief that The Whole Thing is in the process of turning itself off.

But what is it that is doomed? The ego. The question is what reality, what importance, does ego really have? It is something we learned how to do to ourselves, a trick we learned to play, a role we took on, to enable us to grow up and get on with life. But it is a metaphor. When it is gone, we dare say that it was never there at all.

We figured out the same thing about "God" earlier. It's a metaphor. Maybe we needed it to get civilization going, and maybe we didn't. But we made up the metaphor, and we used it. It's as if "God" was the cosmic counterpart of ego. "God" is the ego of the universe. Not really there. A metaphor.

Religions, with their gods or "God," preserve ego,

promising life everlasting, with feasting in paradise with scantily clad young women, looking over the ramparts of heaven and watching and enjoying the sufferings of the damned. In contrast Philosophy, when done seriously, helps us transcend ego, taking us beyond ego.

Let us confront our Dread head-on. Let's really be realists. If we need to construct myths in order to carry us through, let us get busy and do it. But let us not allow other people to deceive us with their myths, which are designed to make us serve them, as their warriors, their cannon fodder, their consumers, cogs on their wheels.

We can get beyond ego and beyond that cosmic ego, "God." We can learn to trust The Whole Thing. We can let go of our little egos and our futile attempts to be in control. We can even learn to quit insisting on results that make us look good. We can quit trusting in the principles of marketing and publicity. We can arrive at uncertainty and learn to enjoy. We can learn to fly.

By now ego is stopping its ears, yelling at the reader to shut the book, calling both author and reader insane, telling the reader to be practical and realistic, ordering the reader to get back into position and obey. For myself, freedom is much better than obeying the frantic ego.

C. The Group

Occasionally I encounter persons with whom I worked back when "God" ran our lives. Some of them also have found their way out of all of that. Some of those who are now out tell me that they miss "the group" and feel that they need it or some sort of substitute for it.

Mostly I miss the group like I miss a toothache after it stops hurting. The church groups constituted a pressure on me that I'm very glad to be without. I do admit that sometimes I miss the singing.

Perhaps I'm a victim of too much study of church history and too many well-remembered personal anecdotes that support the notion that that history is primarily one of organized cruelty. I thought of writing a book of the anecdotes, interspersed with some of the highlights of all that bloody history, but I wondered what would be the use of it in this day and age. **Stories Not for the Squeamish**.

[1] The AIDS patient confesses to his priest that he is gay, and the priest excommunicates him on the spot. The young man is distraught, believing that he is cut off from God, and dies two weeks later.

[2] A western European Christian army marches to the east, to a land they call "holy" because Abraham and Jesus walked there. They plan to take possession of the land and kill all the people who have been living there for

more than a thousand years. On the way they besiege, and then burn down, Constantinople, a city full of Christians, the capital of the Eastern Roman Empire and a trade rival of Venice, another city full of Christians.

[3] The local priest refuses to bury the infant who died in his crib in the night, because the family was behind on their church assessment payments. The family is deeply troubled as they bury the infant without ceremony.

[4] The church/state power executes or exiles all persons of learning, numbering in the many thousands, and then refers to the historical period that follows as "The Dark Ages."

[5] The young missionary pastor opens the Christmas box from the wealthy church back east and pulls out pieces of torn and soiled men's underwear. He burns the entire box.

[6] The TV evangelist announces from the sex offenders prison that if he doesn't preach next Sunday, millions of people will go to hell.

[7] The priest sells a piece of paper which allows the bearer to be excused from one million years in Purgatory.

[8] The zealous young pastor berates the Santa Claus myth relentlessly and convincingly, frightening the children and angering the adults in the congregation. "To teach a falsehood to the young is to lie," he rants, "and telling lies to the young is wrong." The congregation gets rid of him shortly afterward.

[9] Another TV evangelist asks his audience, "How much is eternity worth to you?" committing the crime, if not the sin, of blackmail, equating himself with the Keeper of the Gate, and allowing himself the privilege of charging

admission.

[10] The priests bless the conquerors, who then enslave the conquered population, if they consent to convert to Christianity. The ones who refuse to convert are murdered. The books of the conquered civilization are destroyed, and the lore and the language itself are lost.

[11] The priests turn the crank and the young heretic, accused of witchcraft, feels her back bones separate.

[12] In a public debate over the Vietnam War, the young pastor is stunned when the most honored and respected pastor in the Presbytery tells him that he has no difficulty imagining situations in which Jesus would approve of dropping bombs on little children.

And so forth. It will never become a best-seller.

I left the group because of a felt need to remove myself from all that history and the doctrine behind it. Perhaps not everyone who discovers freedom from God will be quite so badly traumatized. Some will no doubt have had worse experiences.

But the group question comes up continually, and my former colleagues are admitting something that I may not have thought about enough yet. They admit to needing what they called simply "the group."

Humans are mammals, primates, social animals. We define who we are by noting our connections to other humans. Without other people one single human isn't anybody.

We all begin our lives in families. We can't survive without the care of the group. I suspect that our species would not have survived the ice ages, what with sabre-toothed tigers, and the tendency of helpless human infants to cry at the wrong time, if we had not been in fairly cohesive groups.

Humans hunted in bands. The groups became larger and became tribes, in which each one knew who he was because of his identity within the tribe.

Very fine. So we need the group, perhaps in some basic animal sense. But we don't have functioning tribes in modern western civilization. We have families, but the family as a cultural institution is in trouble. We have cults, which are humans bound together by a commonly-held belief system and a shared ritual. We have established churches, official and unofficial, with old and not-so-old traditions, which help us find identifying labels. He's a Baptist. She's a Catholic. He's a Seventh Day Adventist.

Most people nowadays are none of these. We have ethnic origins, and if discrimination is operating, we can comfortably identify with our oppressed group. We have nations, but when the nation becomes overly important and overly demanding, we have nationalism, chauvinism, jingoism and war.

We have economic classes, layers of rank in society, determined mostly now simply by wealth. In our own time and place we're supposed to pretend that we don't have those class distinctions. That is a ploy on the part of the owning class, designed to prevent or forestall what deep down they fear a great deal — class conflict. Karl Marx explained it perfectly clearly, and that's what capitalists don't like about Marx. He explained capitalism. At the moment this teaching which the owning class foists on the others is working very well. Workers are not proud of the fact that they are workers. They wish they didn't have to work. The coupon-clippers are proud that they don't have to exert any labor.

What are free spirits to do in this situation? We have found freedom from "God." We don't need an institution to connect us to "God" and tell us what to do or think. Where is our group? Is this a problem?

There is a spirit which keeps breaking into manifestation, breaking the strangle-hold of the institution or institutions in power. The New Testament Christians embodied that spirit, threatening the powers that ran the Roman Empire. Then organization set in and it hardened and petrified and became in turn a manifestation of Hold Fast — what Rome had been earlier. But that spirit breaks out, time after time. Franciscans, Waldensians, Hussites, Lutherans, Mennonites, Quakers, Methodists, Marxists, socialists, humanists, feminists, environmentalists — each one begins as a challenge to Hold Fast, and then grows and gets organized and turns into an aspect of Hold Fast.

We free spirits will almost certainly be sucked into some modern-day expression of that spirit. We may not join a congealing institution. Most likely we'll be found in Ad Hoc Committees, and it is remarkable how often we'll find ourselves working through one committee or another in opposition to something. U.S. policy toward Colombia, for example. U.S. policy in Iraq. U.S. policy in Haiti. That much alone will keep sensitive free spirits busy. U.S. policy regarding nuclear weapons. U.S. policy on nuclear waste disposal. I'm impressed that so much of what the U.S. Government still has unlimited amounts of money for is what must be opposed. Hold Fast is holding fast.

The Ad Hoc Committee is our group. It can be a very time-consuming commitment. And I must admit to having a serious problem. It's merely a quirk of mine, and hardly worth noting, but I find I must mention it, perhaps as a warning to others. "Meetings," simply meetings as such, make me very uneasy, almost ill. I'm sure it's because I attended, and "led," too many meetings back when I was suffering from the God-obsession. Now meetings feel like such a waste of time and effort, when there's so much work to do.

I know it's my problem, and a contradiction to my own awareness of the tasks confronting sensitive people. Those terrible tasks — trying to save the world from the activities of the U.S. military-industrial monster — won't get done except by humans working in groups. We don't need the group to define for us what we believe or how we are to behave. If the group is still doing that, then we are not yet free. But the tasks that desperately need to be done will have to be done by groups, and we free spirits will have to take part. Abused children, elderly people, the homeless, runaways, whales and dolphins, victims of violence, wetlands, refugees, hungry people, poisoned people, depressed people, sick people, wilderness, the besieged environment itself — individuals acting alone can have little effect on any of that. It will take group action.

But that is spelling out how the groups that are doing all those necessary things need us. How do we need the group? Do we?

We begin in families. For many, for most, the family remains a group. I have become a little sanguine about the family, I must admit. Freedom from God loosened that obligation, too. The gene pool, by itself, is not enough. I am more committed to a series of friends, a surrogate family that has formed, and I am more trustful of them and dependent on them, than I am of the gene pool.

Surrogate families are all around us. Some of us have benefitted greatly from therapy groups and encounter groups. They have sustained us, healed us, better than family ever did. In fact, in some cases what we needed healing from was family.

A teen-age gang is a substitute family. Not far from here one of the gangs calls itself, simply, "Family." They claim turf, and snarl at outsiders — I've seen them do it.

The men's lodge is a sort of family. The social club can be a kind of family. The craft guild was a sort of family and still is. Fellow-artists, fellow-potters, fellow-teachers, fellow-writers. For myself these groups have been far from satisfying. I suspect it's because jealousy rears her ugly head everywhere.

What I already referred to as my "circle of friends" is my family, my group. I'm ready to suppose that everyone needs one, needs some kind of group to trust, to belong to, to share with, and to be simply oneself with.

I was lucky. Not long after leaving the ecclesiastical group, I found my soul mate, and we formed a group of two. For a while it felt like it was us against the world. "There's two of us, and there's only one of them," I used to say. However, we found our group expanding. There were some friends, and even some family, that refused to be driven away, when most were fleeing.

I continued teaching school for several years, and membership on the faculty constituted a sort of ad hoc guild group. Then I quit "to write," and a long period as a loner began. After ten years I formed a publishing company in order to self-publish some of my writing. Without planning, or even ever dreaming of it, the publishing venture grew in such a way that I was publishing other people's work. They needed my help, and I gave it.

Then gradually, without my noticing it, the "stable" of writers I had published became a group. The artist who does all our covers along with two of the authors have become with me an unofficial editorial board. I find myself continually very grateful and more and more dependent on them. A healthy sort of interdependent group seems to have taken form.

The story of one of our titles illustrates this point about the group. Michelle came to me with a proposal. She had been having such a hard time getting through the holidays, lacking three things she regarded as essential:

[1] love, both family and romantic,

[2] money, for feasting and presents and travel and all that, and

[3] some spiritual connection to the meaning of Christmas, "preferably of the Christian type." She had none of the three. "We need to prepare an anthology of writing about this down side of Christmas," she said. "I even have the title — **Christmas Blues**."

Well, characters in my plays, one after another, have been muttering, or shouting, "I hate Christmas!" long enough and often enough, that I instantly agreed that we should do it.

We put out a call for manuscripts. We extended the

deadline several times, rather than attack the growing pile
of material. We stalled and almost dropped the project.
Then we took on Zelda as a fellow-editor. It was a
brilliant move. Her organizational skills and talent as critic
and editor galvanized the other two of us, and it came to
pass — **Christmas Blues: Behind the Holiday Mask.**
Zelda's subtitle is a perfect description of what that
collection of 64 pieces does. It exposes what many can
hardly face. The material took shape in five sections:
Tradition, Family, Outsiders, Stuff, and Remythologizing.
The material was ready to go to the printer. We sent
galleys to six experts, asking for 50-word "blurbs." Two
of them, one in philosophy and one in family medicine,
stunned us with their two-page rave responses. "You have
panned gold!" "It is an immensely healing work."

And so it is. It healed us, the editors. Sixty additional
kindred spirits, all outstanding in their candid honesty and
their irrepressible humor, became an extended group. And
now grateful readers begin to turn up, enlarging the
group. It is a very fine feeling. "If I'd had this book ten
years ago, I wouldn't have blown a thousand dollars on a
trip to Algiers, just to escape the season." We do not
intend to organize, with membership lists and dues and
by-laws. But we are a group, a microcosm of humanity
itself. And I'm able to admit to myself that I need it.
Loner no longer, and I'm thankful.

Conclusion — Still Learning

I feel a strong inclination to share what I'm still learning by sharing what I've been reading. A book is a marvelous thing, and books were the instruments that moved me on my journey toward freedom. I ranged far and wide, over decades, with no Guide. Often I stumbled on what I needed at just the right time, and what felt like happenstance wove it all together in a marvelous way. A sort of magic occurred often in used book stores! Sometimes I found a book but then kept it on hold for a while, sometimes a very long while. And then a word, a reference, some little chance thing, would move the book up to the top of the pile.

But I wonder why I should tell that story. I'm sure you don't need to learn the tiny percentage of what-there-is-to-know that I happen to know. Yet perhaps it could be helpful, so I am willing to share my list. Take it as an item from the For-Whatever-It's-Worth Department.

We have to be at it all the time, all our lives, this attempt to figure out what's going on. This journey is filled with such wonders; those who brag with their bumper stickers that they've "found it" reveal only their closed minds. We've found a lot, but we're also still searching, examining pebbles on the beach, with an ocean right there, as Darwin said.

Of all the poets, William Blake opened me up the most. His invention of the word, "Nobodaddy," was alone worth any effort I expended.

I read a great deal of the classic psychological writings of Sigmund Freud, Erich Fromm and Karl Jung. Fromm is easiest to follow, and makes the most useful sense:

The Art of Loving
Man for Himself
The Heart of Man
The Sane Society
The Forgotten Language.

The last title led to myths and dreams. Joseph Campbell became my mentor. I found him long before Bill Moyers made his name a household word.

Hero with a Thousand Faces
The Masks of God (four volumes)
Myths, Dreams and Religion
Myths to Live By.

I taught high school seniors from **Hero with a Thousand Faces** and gained much more than they did from the exercise. **Memories, Dreams and Reflections**, by Karl Jung, is a classic which simply "blew my mind," to use the phrase my students used at the time.

When I said I had no guide, I over-simplified. I taught school for ten years, and I was one of those teachers who allowed my students to guide much of my reading. I mean, I was prescribing a fair amount of theirs! In every semester, there were a few, mostly sixth-graders, who brought me the books that excited them. I promised I would read whatever they brought me, and I did. That's how I found the fairy tales, and many Children's Classics that I had missed as a child. If you have children or students or nieces or nephews or grandchildren, pay attention to what they tell you about reading. Let a little child lead. I did, and it did me a world of good. I'm referring to reading, not TV shows and not videos.

Thanks to those kids I read all the books I could lay my hands on with titles like:

Fairy Tales from (wherever)

Legends of the (whoever)

Children's Stories from (wherever).

They also helped me find:

The Yearling, Rawlings

The Pushcart War, Merrill

A Wrinkle in Time, L'Engle

When the Legends Die, Borland

The Light in the Forest, Richter

The Moon is Down, Steinbeck

The Snow Goose, Gallico

Tales Told near a Crocodile, Harman

Noodles, Nitwits and Numskulls, Leach

I Never Saw Another Butterfly, children from the concentration camp at Terezin.

Alan Watts introduced me to the philosophies of the Orient:

The Spirit of Zen

The Way of Zen

The Joyous Cosmology

The Two Hands of God

Myth and Ritual in Christianity

The Book.

The last title is very valuable for arriving at an

understanding of one's own ego.

Zen and yoga have been worth all the time I have put on them. My wife and I do Tai Chih every morning — it is our "body work." We believe that everyone needs something of that sort. Our Western Christian tradition neglected it, and jogging or workouts in a gymnasium seem so violent when compared to the Chinese technique of "activating the energy and balancing the energy."

Jonathan Swift called science a prostitute in **Gulliver's Travels.** I highly recommend Gulliver in the original, not something edited by Sunday School teachers for over-protected children! As far as science is concerned, Swift is right. Many scientists all over the world have indeed sold their ingenuity and their knowledge and any commitment to truth to the highest bidders, first the Pentagon or the Kremlin, and now assorted profit-making corporations. But not all scientists are doing for money what they should do for love — that is seek Truth. The best thinkers in this field still love this planet more than money. Loren Eiseley, and his successor, for me, Lewis Thomas, have found very important overarching meaning in all the scientific data now available.

The Immense Journey, Eiseley

Lives of a Cell, Thomas

William Kaufman's, **Faith of a Heretic**, helped me greatly at break-away time. Harvey Cox, who didn't break away, helped recently with **The Seduction of the Spirit**, written more than ten years ago. I was just thinking, if what he's writing can still be called "theology," what am I writing? Anti-theology, some will want to call it.

I must comment on the Bible. In the hands of those

mean-hearted closed-minded people you can see on TV, it is a weapon used to bludgeon sensitive and sensible people into a disgusted silence. And those same people often conclude that the Bible is worthless, or worse. It's similar to letting the warmongers have science and the computer, just because they, so far, have made the most dramatic use of those tools.

The Bible is the root of the myth of our Western Civilization. That myth is now widely regarded as irrelevant and/or erroneous, and/or harmful. But simple and complete rejection of that myth, or all myth, leaves us with no myth. That leaves us with no roots, no values that go back anywhere, no stories that connect anyone with anyone, no meaning in anything. That makes us susceptible, purely by default, to the violent, macho, trashy, imperialistic, insensitive garbage which fills the airwaves in our time. It creates the sociopaths that frighten us so. People will have myth — we can't get by without it. Man is the myth-making animal.

I, for one anyway, find it worthwhile to take up the task of remythologization, using the Bible as one of the important sources. To the extent that the "Bible-message" is divisive, non-universal, non-planetary, sexist, or racist in outlook, it is in error. In such instances it is ethnocentric and merely Hebrew, or sectarian and merely Christian. But much of the Bible is also merely human, and thus still everyone's material.

There is no doubt that the effort required to master some of the difficulties is considerable. The need to master two ancient languages, Hebrew and Greek, is a formidable starter, but let's get at it. Otherwise we have another baby that is often thrown out with the bath.

Some heavy tomes in other fields of enquiry have done me much good. Your list will be different.

Gödel, Escher, Bach, Hofstadter
Metamagical Themas, Hofstadter
The Tao of Physics, Capra
The Dancing Wu-Li Masters, Zukav
Origin and History of Consciousness, Neumann
The Great Mother, Neumann
The Uses of Enchantment, Bettleheim
Women Who Run with the Wolves, Estes
Writing down the Bones, Goldberg
The Aquarian Conspiracy, Ferguson
Cosmic Consciousness, Bucke
Being Red, Fast
The Holographic Universe, Talbot
The Zen of Seeing, Franck
The Occult, Wilson
The Outsider, Wilson
The Denial of Death, Becker
The Unfinished Universe, Young
The Cry for Myth, May

Recently I found myself attracted primarily to biographies, and autobiographies. At one point I had a vague question in the back of my mind. "What does a well-lived human life consist of?" I thought at the time that my advancing age and the perspective it allows helped me in formulating that question. I have read heavy books which document the lives of many fascinating persons, including: Henry Adams, Mahatma Gandhi, Michelangelo, Francis of Assisi, Eugenio Pacelli, Albino Luciani,

Yogananda, William Wallace, Robert the Bruce, Aaron Burr, Abraham Lincoln, Woodrow Wilson, Vincent Van Gogh, Salvador Dali, Sigmund Freud, Hadley Hemingway, Anton Chekhov, Aldous Huxley, William Shirer, Howard Fast, Martha Gellhorn, Henry Miller, Wilhelm Reich, Walt Whitman, Loren Eiseley, Lillian Hellman, Annie Dillard, Gabriel Garcia Marquez. There seems to be no simple answer to the question above, about human life, but it's been an adventure of sharing, in any case.

Living a human life is a mystery. I have found that it is even more mysterious now than when "God" provided pat answers to very deep and important questions. Living free is an on-going process, an adventure in which learning never ends.

Other Thought-provoking Books
from Amador Publishers:

Ancestral Notes: a Family Dream Journal,
Zelda Leah Gatuskin, ISBN: 0-938513-17-6,
175 pp. $10

Try to reject your personal heritage. The ancestors won't allow it. This multi-media masterpiece explores what it means to be a Jew, to be a woman, and to be a member of the human race.

Vermin and Other Survival Stories: Humanity as an Endangered Species, Harry Willson; ISBN: 0-938513-22-2 192 pp. $10

Plutonium, radioactive materials in sewers, air conditioners, nuclear waste storage, overpopulation, fundamentalism, and satire itself — all are fair game in these stories, fables, essays and exposés.

Christmas Blues: Behind the Holiday Mask,
An Anthology; ISBN: 0-938513-18-4, 352 pp. $15

Stories, essays and poems explore the down side of the holidays. Some are whimsical, some bitter, some funny, some disgusting — all are so honest they have a healing effect. Everyone knows someone who needs this book.

The Pianist Who Liked Ayn Rand, Gene H. Bell-Villada; ISBN: 0-938513-24-9, 256 pp. $14

How far will up-front self-centeredness get you? The title story tells all. Other stories range from minimalism, wistfulness and fantasy to bitter satire. Very provoking.

A World for the Meek: a Fantasy Novel,
Harry Willson; ISBN: 0-938513-01-X, 192 pp. $9

A post-blast, life-affirming fantasy. Noah thinks he's the last man in the world, until the dolphins find him. They think they've found a live fossil. He is delighted that they let him into their world.

Hunger in the First Person Singular, Michelle Miller; ISBN: 0-938513-15-X, 170 pp. $9

"This is a power piece that goes straight for your emotional and sexual jugular." A ghost town hermit records her four years in isolation. A man (her animus?) appears, leaving mysterious and puzzling clues to his presence. A profound and bewildering journey of mind, body and spirit ensues.

Undercurrents: New Mexico Stories Then and Now, Adela Amador; ISBN: 0-938513-27-3, 176 pp. $12

Full of anecdotes in the style of the Spanish *cuento*, this collection celebrates permanence and change, and casts light on the lives of the varied peoples of New Mexico over many decades. Beneath a placid-seeming surface, deep undercurrents are flowing. "She writes with her heart on the point of her pen."

AMADOR PUBLISHERS
P. O. Box 12335
Albuquerque, NM 87195
Phone/FAX 505-877-4395
To Order: 800-730-4395
e-mail   harry@amadorbooks.com
http://www.amadorbooks.com

ORDER BLANK

of copies   price

_____ FREEDOM FROM GOD   @ 15.00_____

_____ ANCESTRAL NOTES   @ 10.00_____

_____ VERMIN   @ 10.00_____

_____ CHRISTMAS BLUES   @ 15.00_____

_____ PIANIST WHO LIKED
        AYN RAND   @ 14.00_____

_____ A WORLD FOR THE MEEK   @ 9.00_____

_____ HUNGER IN THE FIRST
        PERSON SINGULAR   @ 9.00_____

_____ UNDERCURRENTS   @ 12.00_____

_____ SOULS AND CELLS
        REMEMBER   @ 8.00_____

    postage & handling   2.00

    Total   _____

Send to: Name_____

      Address_____